Books by Kenneth Koch

POETRY

One Train   1994
On the Great Atlantic Rainway, Selected Poems 1950–1988   1994
Seasons on Earth   1987
On the Edge   1986
Selected Poems: 1950–1982   1985
Days and Nights   1982
The Burning Mystery of Anna in 1951   1979
The Duplications   1977
The Art of Love   1975
The Pleasures of Peace   1969
When the Sun Tries to Go On   1969
Poems from 1952 and 1953   1968
Thank You and Other Poems   1962
Permanently   1961
Ko, or A Season on Earth   1960

FICTION

Hotel Lambosa   1993
The Red Robins   1975

THEATER

The Gold Standard: A Book of Plays   1996
One Thousand Avant-Garde Plays   1988
The Red Robins   1979
A Change of Hearts   1973
Bertha and Other Plays   1966

EDUCATIONAL WORKS

Sleeping on the Wing:
    An Anthology of Modern Poetry with Essays on Reading and Writing
    (with Kate Farrell)   1981
I Never Told Anybody:
    Teaching Poetry Writing in a Nursing Home   1977
Rose, Where Did You Get That Red?:
    Teaching Great Poetry to Children   1973
Wishes, Lies, and Dreams:
    Teaching Children to Write Poetry   1970

THE
GOLD
STANDARD

KENNETH KOCH

Alfred A. Knopf New York 1996

THE
GOLD
STANDARD

A Book of Plays

THIS IS A BORZOI BOOK
PUBLISHED BY ALFRED A. KNOPF, INC.

Most of the plays in this collection were previously published in the following:

A Heroine of the Greek Resistance in *American Poetry Review,* Sept.–Oct. 1994, Vol. 23, No. 5. The first speech of this play (lines 1-22) was the text of a book made in collaboration with the French artist Bertrand Dorny, in 1993, entitled *The Tee Shirt.*

The Strangers from the Sea in *Arshile,* 1995, no. 4.

The Banquet in *Boulevard,* Summer 1996, Vol. 11.

Edward and Christine is based on *Hotel Lambosa,* a book of short stories published by Coffee House Press, Minneapolis, in 1993.

The Red Robins was originally published by Performing Arts Journal Publications, New York, in 1979.

George Washington Crossing the Delaware and *The Construction of Boston* were originally published in *Bertha and Other Plays,* Grove Press, New York, in 1966. *The Gold Standard* was originally published in *A Change of Hearts* by Random House, Inc., New York, in 1973.

http://www.randomhouse.com/

Library of Congress Cataloging-in-Publication Data

Koch, Kenneth

    The gold standard : plays / Kenneth Koch.

      p. cm.

    ISBN 0-679-45082-3

    I. Title.

PS3521.027G65   1996

812′.54—dc20   96-26169

                              CIP

Manufactured in the United States of America
First Edition

In memory of Jean-Claude Vignes

ACKNOWLEDGMENTS

My thanks to Jordan Davis who helped me put this book together, and to Karen Koch, who listened to a lot of it, and to the directors and actors who put on my plays so well that I have kept wanting to write more of them.

CONTENTS

THE
GOLD
STANDARD

THE GOLD STANDARD *was first produced at Saint Peter's Church Theatre, New York, in 1975, directed by Robert Gainer.*

A mountain shrine in China, Enter two MONKS.

FIRST MONK:

> Sit down. Now let us rest the burden here
> Of our exhausted mortal parts and speak
> Of things we do not understand. Commence.

SECOND MONK:

> Oft have I wondered when I hear men say
> That in their land the currency is solid
> Because it rests upon a base of gold.
> They call it . . .

FIRST MONK:

> The gold standard—

SECOND MONK:

> Yes, that's it!
> And often on some lonely winter night
> Which freezes traveler and his poor mount
> Who, wandering down some valley side, know not
> Which way to turn so as to find their rest,
> Oft have I heard men's conversation turn
> To gold and to that system too whereby
> The currency of any nation may
> Be given a solid base

FIRST MONK:

> By the gold standard.

SECOND MONK:

>   Yes, "gold standard." But you who seem to understand
>   Such fiscal matters, tell me now and briefly
>   What this gold-standard fiscal system is.

FIRST MONK:

>   That I shall try, though of success be never sure
>   Till it has come unquestioned. Shall not I
>   Use for example the United States
>   For there I know the gold is in Fort Knox
>   And all their currency is based on it?

SECOND MONK:

>   It's well. Proceed.

FIRST MONK:

>   Proceed to it I shall.
>   But where shall I begin? Perhaps with coin,
>   Yes that is where I should begin, because
>   It's there the question rises. Let me see.
>   If I have here a token in my hand
>   Of wood or metal, and we say that it
>   Is "worth five dollars," then what can we mean?

SECOND MONK:

>   What is a dollar? Tell me that before
>   You carry any further this great theme.

FIRST MONK:

>   It is the coin of the United States.
>   One says one dollar, two dollars, five dollars,
>   Ten dollars, twenty dollars, ninety dollars,
>   And so on to a billion. As for smaller
>   Denominations, they are parts of dollars—
>   A nickel, for example, is one-twentieth
>   Part of a dollar, and a dime one-tenth
>   A penny is a hundredth part, a quarter
>   A quarter part as one might well expect.
>   There is among the coins also another,
>   The half-dollar—and now my list's complete.

4

So when I say one dollar now you will
Know what I mean? or when I say a dime?

SECOND MONK:

Perhaps I'd better have a record of it.
Have you a plume? I'll write these figures down.
Yes, now, that's it, I think I understand
And if I do not I can look that up
Upon the list which I forget to know.

FIRST MONK:

Fine, now we have the list and have begun.
Thus to more difficult matters. If I have
A token in my hand of which 'tis said
That is five dollars, in what sense can that
Be said to have a meaning? that is to say,
Why should you give me, if I give you this,
This token that I say is worth five dollars,
Why should you give me rice, and fish, and ink?

SECOND MONK:

Because you are my brother, Cho Fu San,
And I would not deny you anything.

FIRST MONK:

I asked here for a monetary reason.
I know, Kai Fong, there is not anything
We'd not do for each other—but if I,
A stranger to you, held this token out,
Why should you give me meat or fish for it?

SECOND MONK (*smiling*):

Why, I would recognize you, Cho Fu San—
That scar upon your hand which healed the cut
You got in gathering branches in last year
So we could make the fire at Ho Ku Temple
Where they had for a time run out of fuel.
You were much praised for that. Could I forget
A deed so noble or a hand so marred
By what it did for selflessness? Besides,
Even if you had no scar upon that hand,

What if I did not know your name or face,
What if you came to me and asked for fish
And held a token out—would I not give?
Is not our duty still toward all who need?

FIRST MONK:

    I now perceive
How far the concept of all payment is
From your enlightened soul. Yet I'll explain
In a more fundamental way, so that
You may perceive it clearly—for, who knows?
Such knowledge may empower us some day
To do some good we do not know of now.
Attend! You know in the non-priestly world
That men instead of bartering, that is,
Giving a fish for rice, or trees for seed,
Or wives for cattle, or spun silk for tea
Have worked a system out in which there is
Some kind of general substance which is used
To represent the barter value of
Each kind of thing one needs.

SECOND MONK:

    I do not know
Exactly what you mean by "value," brother.

FIRST MONK:

    Explain.

SECOND MONK:

    Well, if I give you green tea leaves,
Say half a pound of them and you give me
In fair exchange three pounds of rice, shall not
We say, then, that the "value" of a pound
Of rice can be computed at one-third
A half-pound of green tea?

FIRST MONK:

    That is, one sixth,
Yes, one sixth of a pound of green tea leaves

6

Would be the "value" of a pound of rice.
You seem to me to understand the concept.

SECOND MONK:

Wait! If another brother, passing by,
Has urgent need of rice, and offers me
Six pounds of green tea leaves for what I have,
What is the "value" of the green tea then
And of the pound of rice?

FIRST MONK:

The pound of rice
Is worth six pounds of green tea leaves.

SECOND MONK:

Then you,
If you should wish to buy your own rice back,
Would find that with your half a pound of tea
You could buy but one-twelfth of a pound of rice.
If then you wished some tea along with rice
And tried to purchase some green tea from me
At what we had agreed to be the "value"
Of half a pound of tea, you would receive
For all your rice but one-twelfth of one-sixth
Of one pound of green tea, which is, I think,
One seventy-second of a pound of tea.
Then if you tried to buy some rice from him
Who had the rice you sold him, and perhaps
By chance had now some more, for all your tea
You would receive, I must take plume and paper,
One seventy-two times six, four thirty-second,
One four hundred and thirty-second part
Of a pound of rice is all you would receive.
Then if you wished—

FIRST MONK:

Stop, brother! you are driving me insane!
I have not followed you. I am all lost
In these fine figurings. Let me begin
Another way, that all shall not be lost.

SECOND MONK:

    Lost surely to you were much rice and tea
    In what I figured out, which I imagine
    Was accurately tuned to what you'd said.
    Perhaps all currency is chaos—

FIRST MONK:

    No,
    Let me explain again. At least I'll try.
    For night is going past.
    And we, in this part of the subject, are
    Still far from understanding what the "base"
    Of currency may be, and how a standard
    Of gold or silver can sustain its value.

SECOND MONK:
    But "value"—

FIRST MONK:

    Kai Fong, I said that I would try.
    I know that "value" is not clear just yet
    And yet it is an ordinary concept
    Which I am certain we can understand
    Together, let me but find the proper words.
    In the example that you gave just now,
    You spoke of two discreet ideas of value—
    For me, the rice was worth less than the tea,
    And so for you, at the time of our exchange.

SECOND MONK:

    Yes, I can vouch for that. For you gave me
    For three whole pounds of rice only one half
    A pound of green tea leaves.

FIRST MONK:

    But this was done
    By our agreement; we did not dispute
    The value of these things.

SECOND MONK:
    Yes, for the sake

8

Of finishing our discussion, let us say
That we agreed, although I do not remember
How we agreed, or why.

FIRST MONK:

Then let us say,
That we agreed and that there was a reason
We came to this agreement, which was this:
That there is only a given amount of rice
In China and a given amount of tea.

SECOND MONK:

The man who can find out such vast amounts
Must be some sort of Buddha at the least—
For who could know such things?

FIRST MONK:

Why, men may go
To all the villages and ask each man
How much of rice he has and how much tea.

SECOND MONK:

But this would take a thousand thousand years.
China is vast.

FIRST MONK:

True—and perhaps there is no need
To go to every village in the country—
Perhaps it is enough to know how much
Rice and tea there are in one's own village.
Then, if one finds there are ten thousand pounds
Of rice, and fifteen thousand pounds of tea,
One can compute that for one pound of rice
One should receive a pound and a half of tea.

SECOND MONK:

Yes, I have checked it with my plume
And paper, and I find you are correct.

FIRST MONK:

Thus can each village figure for itself

9

The price of rice in tea or tea in rice.
Then if, say, Village Chu should be the one
In which one pound of rice is worth of tea
One pound and a half, and if in Village Cheng
There were eighteen thousand pounds of rice and nine
Thousand pounds of tea, so that for one
Pound of rice one got one half-pound of tea,
Then it would be in the interests of the men of Chu
To take their tea to Cheng and sell it there;
So men of Cheng would sell their rice in Chu.
Eventually there would be established
A common rate for rice and tea which was
Observed in Cheng and Chu.

SECOND MONK:

Which I suppose
Would be—let's see—the total of the rice
In both towns is twenty-eight thousand pounds,
Of the tea twenty-four thousand—both can be
Divided, seven to six. Yes tea would be
Worth one and one-sixth pounds of rice per pound.

FIRST MONK:

See what a brilliant light the moon throws now
Upon our humble floor of straw and reeds!
So man by guidance of superior light
May understand his world.

SECOND MONK:

And we may see
How little we have fathomed yet of all
We have set out to know. Distant still seems
The goal of understanding this our subject.
For what has gold to do with where we are now?

FIRST MONK:

If it is decided
That for one pound of tea one can receive
One and a sixth pounds of rice, then one can say
Let this wood token serve to represent

One-sixth of a pound of rice. With six of these
One can obtain a pound of rice, with seven
One can obtain a pound of tea.

SECOND MONK:

But why
Would anyone take that which "represents"
In change for that which is? A sketch in ink
May "represent" this mountain, yet I would not
Take it in fair exchange.

FIRST MONK:

Of "represent"
Two meanings are there—other is the one
I took than that which you have understood.
And yet it serves to introduce the next
Step in the argument that binds us here.

SECOND MONK:

I wished to know, since I cannot eat wood
But must eat rice, why I would take this wood
And give good rice for it.

FIRST MONK:

The reason is
That for "this wood," if given in a trade
You could receive the same amount of rice
You traded for the wood. Of, if you wished,
Six sevenths of a pound of tea.

SECOND MONK:

And yet,
What if I traded all my tea for wood
And all my rice for wood, then had much wood,
A thousand thousand thousand pounds of wood
And what if no one wished to have my wood,
Would I turn termite then to eat my wood
Or would I simply starve for lack of rice
And die of thirst for lack of steaming tea
Which fills the soul with purpose and delight

And reverence for all being? I should not,
I think, give any of my rice for wood
Or any of my tea.

FIRST MONK:

    The deepest shades
Of ebony-black night by now are past;
Some stars are gone; few others through the fog
Are shining still; much time does not remain
Till we once more, at dawning, must descend
Into the hills and valleylands below.
I wish, before that come, that on this night
Some further understanding yet might be
Generously given us by One above.
Perhaps I see a way: what if this wood,
Which I agree with you necessity
Would not require to be desired by many
And certainly not all, what if this token
Were made, instead, of gold?

SECOND MONK:

    A thing of beauty!
A rare thing also! I would gladly give
Some tea or rice for it, for then I could
Carve a sweet Buddha from it which I'd place
In great Gautama's honor in some shrine!

FIRST MONK:

    We have not yet
Arrived at this great argument's full course!
New difficulties show at every turn
And we must show brave hearts to carry on!
What if you did not make a statuette
Of all this gold you had, but if you kept it
And used it, some perhaps for sculpturing,
But other pieces of it to buy tea
And rice and clothing, to acquit yourself
Of every human need, nor be obliged
To carry rice and tea around with you
To barter for each single thing you wanted?

Would that not be a great convenience
And joy and boon to man?

SECOND MONK:

    I think I see.
The gold would "represent" the rice and tea
Yet also have a value of its own.

FIRST MONK:

    Yes, and all persons would agree on it.

SECOND MONK:

    What if some person should not care for gold?

FIRST MONK:

    Why, he would learn he could get tea for it,
So he would treasure it as he did tea.

SECOND MONK:

    I think I see. So by a general process
Of village into village, state through state,
The general value of a pound of tea
Is fixed, as is the value of an ounce
Of gold; but how is gold distributed?
What if a man have only rice and tea?

FIRST MONK:

    Why, he can sell some rice and get some gold.

SECOND MONK:

    But what if no one in the country 'round
Have any gold? What would they use for money?
Would they go back to bartering again?

FIRST MONK:

    I do not know. Perhaps the government
Would have in every village people doing
Governmental jobs for which they'd pay them
In quantities of gold, then gradually
This gold would be distributed about
So that each person had some, and each town.

SECOND MONK:

> If gold were scarce, might not men hoard it then
> And melt it into ingots, from which they
> Might mold great Bodhisattvas fair as heaven?
> And if sufficient number acted so
> There would not be much gold about, and so
> Men would go back to barter once again.

FIRST MONK:

> Too true. The only answer then would be
> To find more gold and turn it into coins.

SECOND MONK:

> And these, in turn, when hoarders got to them
> Would vanish into Buddhas. And besides,
> The supply of gold, you said, was limited.

FIRST MONK:

> We may be closer than we thought we were
> To the chief subject of our argument—
> Which is how gold which is not used can give
> "Value" to coins and paper bills which are.
> Where we are now, it seems to me, is this:
> That there are serious reasons for not using
> Gold as currency; and one is hoarding.

SECOND MONK:

> What might another be?

FIRST MONK:

> Gold wears away.
> It is a metal generally soft.
> With constant use the wealth of any nation
> Would gradually decrease, a sorry thing.

SECOND MONK:

> So paper, then, and other things are used
> In place of gold—but since they have no value,
> Or do not have the value of the gold,
> Why do men count them as if they were gold?

14

FIRST MONK:

> That is the mystery of the gold standard
> Which now we must attempt to understand.

SECOND MONK:

> Cho Fu San, I had a thought.

FIRST MONK:

> What is it, dear Kai Fong?

SECOND MONK:

> It did occur to me that I have heard
> That the United States no longer used
> What we have called gold standard, but instead
> The silver standard for its currency.

FIRST MONK:

> Your words ring true.
> I do remember that that is the case.
> I had forgot. Yet still we have not lost
> These precious hours of night, for I perceive
> We have but one more step to understand
> Once we have seen what the gold standard is.

SECOND MONK:

> What is it, Cho Fu San?

FIRST MONK:

> To understand
> How the gold ingots buried in Fort Knox
> Can guarantee the value of the paper
> In silver, which I think should be quite clear.
> For once one knows how much a pound of silver
> Is worth in gold, then one can calculate
> How much a piece of paper backed by gold
> Embedded in the earth is worth in silver.

SECOND MONK:

> I take it that the silver is not buried
> Instead of gold because, being less precious

They would need more of it, a great deal more,
And thus would have to dig a larger cavern
And labor terribly to carry down
Into the cavern so much weight in silver.

FIRST MONK:

    And, besides,
The huge amount of gold now buried there
Would have to be transported to the surface—
And what, exactly, would they do with it?

SECOND MONK:

    Why, they could give it in exchange to those
Who gave the silver that they placed in earth.

FIRST MONK:

    Would people give the silver? I believe
That they would bury governmental silver.

SECOND MONK:

    How would the government obtain the silver?

FIRST MONK:

    From silver mines belonging to the state.

SECOND MONK:

    Has it much silver now?

FIRST MONK:

    I do not know.
I any case, the gold is buried still
And it is used to guarantee the value
In silver of the paper and the coins.

SECOND MONK:

    Dear Cho Fu San, some aspects yet unclear
Are to my spirit. Why should I accept
A piece of paper for a pound of rice
Because some gold is buried in the earth
Which I can neither use, nor hoard, nor see?

16

FIRST MONK:

    I think perhaps that you would have the right
    At any time to give the government
    The piece of paper and receive the gold.

SECOND MONK:

    What? would they dig it up? Suppose each person
    Should trade in all his paper bills for gold?
    Then there would be no ingots in the earth
    Nor any paper bills. Then we should have
    Gold coins again—

FIRST MONK:

    Perhaps this is the reason
    The country has gone on the silver standard.
    The gold remains to guarantee the value
    Of coins and paper money, but one cannot
    Obtain the gold in fair exchange for it,
    But only silver.

SECOND MONK:

    Where, if not in earth,
    If not in some voluminous Fort Knox,
    Is all the silver kept which would be needed
    To give to everyone in fair exchange
    If all decided to turn in their money
    For silver bars?

FIRST MONK:

    Kai Fong, I do not know.
    Besides, if all these silver bars existed
    What need would be to have the buried gold?
    For silver itself would guarantee the value
    Of every coin and bill.

SECOND MONK:

    Oh Cho Fu San,
    Our cerebrations now must reach an end.
    The morning rises, and the mist that clears
    Reveals a lightsome snow which promises
    A perilous descent. Come on, old friend—

Let those who need possessions puzzle out
The snaggles of this argument. For us,
Who live by other lights, what we have learned
This evening seems enough.

FIRST MONK:

I come, old friend.
The trail is difficult.

SECOND MONK:

Here, take my arm.
We shall find other shelter once below.

END

GEORGE
WASHINGTON
CROSSING
THE DELAWARE

GEORGE WASHINGTON CROSSING THE
DELAWARE *was first produced at the Maidman Playhouse, New York, in March, 1962. Directed by Arthur Storch, decor and costumes by Alex Katz, and with Richard Libertini and MacIntyre Dixon as Washington and Cornwallis.*

SCENE 1

Alpine, New Jersey.

GEORGE WASHINGTON:

General Cornwallis, you cannot stay here in the trails of Alpine, New Jersey. The American army will drive you away, and away! Americans shall be masters of the American continent! Then, perhaps, of the world!

CORNWALLIS:

What tomfoolery is that you speak, George Washington? You are a general, and generals are supposed to have a college education. No man with any sense would see a victory in this conflict for any power but GREAT BRITAIN!

GEORGE WASHINGTON:

General Cornwallis, I am a mild man, but you had better not say that kind of thing to me. I tell you, America shall win the Revolutionary War!

FIRST AIDE TO GEORGE WASHINGTON:

Our general speaks the truth, Englishman.

FIRST AIDE TO CORNWALLIS:

Do you dare to speak to General Cornwallis, impudent Yankee?

FIRST AIDE TO GEORGE WASHINGTON:

Aye, I am an American, and I fear to speak to no man.

GEORGE WASHINGTON:

My aide is expressing the philosophy we all have. It is bound to triumph over your own British authoritarian and colonial system. My men all see eye to eye on this point.

CORNWALLIS:

I caution you, General Washington, that many of them will never see eye to eye with anything again if you persist in this useless, cruel, and wasteful battle.

GEORGE WASHINGTON:

Come, my loyal men. We waste our time in entreaty with the English lord. He mocks us and all we believe.

FIRST AIDE TO GEORGE WASHINGTON:

Aye, General, I follow you.

OTHER AIDES:

Aye, General, we come.

(*They leave.*)

CORNWALLIS:

There goes the greatest man who will ever live in America! If only he could come over to the English side, I could bring myself to give up my command to him. He is a perfect gentleman, excelling in manners as in speech. His dress is perfect, his buttoning neat, and his shoes of a high polish. He speaks frankly and freely, and will say straight out to his most bitter opponent that which is in his mind. There is nothing he could not accomplish, would he but set himself to it. What task, indeed, could ever challenge that general of the Revolutionary Army? He rides as he walks, with perfect grace; and when he reclines, one imagines one sees the stately bison taking its rest among the vast unexplored plains of this country, America, which now in foul and lawless revolt dares to lift its head against its English nurse and mother. What is more unnatural than that this man, Washington, who is one of God's gentlemen, should so defy the laws of right and wrong as to raise his hand against the breast that gave him suck, against the tender maternal care of England? O England, England! we who are your subjects are the most fortunate men on earth, and we shall struggle boldly to defend you, on land and at sea, no matter where we shall find ourselves, in whatever tempest or time of trouble that may come—we shall be, as we are, loyal to the end, and triumph we shall, for love makes our cause right. . . . But that man Washington!

(CONWALLIS *leaves.*)

FIRST AIDE TO CORNWALLIS:
Our general is troubled.

SECOND AIDE TO CORNWALLIS:
The sight of the Yankee general has quite o'erthrown him.

FIRST BRITISH SOLDIER (*cockney accent*):
A did not think 'e was such a great man but I could 'ave ho'ertopped 'im wi' me little musket 'ere. 'Tis bare gaddiness that our general be disturbed.

SECOND BRITISH SOLDIER (*cockney accent*):
Aye, but disturbed 'e is.

THIRD BRITISH SOLDIER (*Irish brogue*):
Come off, now. What is it turns your heads so low, and the sun beatin' back against them, and your steps draggin', and no light of day in your eyes, and here it bein' God's own glorious time, when His Majesty walked in the Garden of Eden, in the cool of the day, and the glorious messenger of Zeus almighty and the eye of friendly Apollo ashinin' and aglistenin' in yonder famous West, where so many of our victories has been? What is there to make a man sad in a time of day such as this is, when all is gold as far as the eye can listen, and where the buzzin' of a thrillion insects shines through the ear? If a man were not happy at such a moment, he were but half a man, and that half not much good neither, but only for changin' and blackin' the pots while old Mother helps herself to some kidneys. It is a glad song I would be singin' but for some that would have it that all men must be sad in the time of the American War. Saw you not General Washington?

FIRST BRITISH SOLDIER (*cockney accent*):
Sawr'im plain, I did, just as big as your 'ead there; troubled a bit, our general is, 'aving seen 'im 'isself. Gaive a nice speech habout Hengland though.

SECOND BRITISH SOLDIER (*cockney accent*):
Aye, troubled 'e is, and deep, too. I see no good of this meetin'.

(*They all leave.*)

23

SCENE 2

The American camp.

FIRST AMERICAN SOLDIER:
The General returns, and surely he will tell us much that he has seen.

SECOND AMERICAN SOLDIER:
When the General goes abroad, he never fails to tell each private soldier, though he be lowest in station in the entire Revolutionary Army, what he, the General, has seen, and what his thoughts have been upon the subjects of his contemplation.

THIRD AMERICAN SOLDIER:
Thus, each and every man in the Revolutionary Army shares in the secrets of the High Command, and every man knows exactly why he is fighting.

FOURTH AMERICAN SOLDIER:
This is democracy in action, actually being practiced in a military situation. The method of our struggle exemplifies its end—freedom for every man from the English.

FIFTH AMERICAN SOLDIER:
Here comes the General!

(GEORGE WASHINGTON *enters and mounts a podium.*)

GEORGE WASHINGTON:
Friends, soldiers, and Americans, lend me your ears!
        (*Laughter.*)
I have seen the British general, Cornwallis—
Brightly he shines in regal uniform,
And brightly shines his sword—but she will cut
No better, boys, than ours!
(*Draws his sword, amid the thunderous cheers of the soldiers.*)
                                        He said that we
Had not a chance at all to win the war. . . .
        (*Laughter.*)
Let's show that Englishman how wrong he is
        (*Growls.*)
And conquer them as quickly as we can! (*Cheers.*)

A RAGGED SOLDIER:

> General Washington, how can we conquer the Englishmen when we have no guns, no ammunition, no clothing, and no food?

> (*Loud murmurs from the soldiers of "Shhhhh shhh," "Strike him," "Why does he want to spoil everything?" "Kill him," etc.*)

GEORGE WASHINGTON (*unruffled*):

> We must make raids—raids, raids,
> Raids on the English supplies. We must make raids!
> Raids for clothing and raids for food
> To do the Revolutionary Army good;
> Raids in the morning and raids at night,
> Raids on our stomachs by candlelight,
> Raids on the tea chest and raids on the mill,
> Raids on the granary that stands by the hill;
> Raids on the clothing tents, beautiful raids,
> Raids on Cornwallis, and raids on his aides.
> For stealing is licensed if for a good cause,
> And in love and in war, boys, you know there're no laws.
> So pack up your shyness, your shame, and your fear,
> And throw them away, and come meet me, all, here,
> At twelve o'clock midnight, and off we shall go
> To the camp of the English that lies down below!
> And we shall return in their splendid attire,
> And every man present shall have his desire.
> So, come, get you ready—go blacken each face,
> And met me at midnight in this very place!

SCENE 3

An English home.

ENGLISH GIRL:

> You mustn't cry, Mummy. There's absolutely nothing we can do. We are in England, and he is in America. Your tears are going to waste. Has he written?

MOTHER:

The poor little fellow. I remember the first step he ever took. His father, may his soul rest in peace, was holding on to his tiny hands; and, when he began to step forward, all by his little self, his daddy let him go. And he took such a tumble! How I kissed him then—oh!

ENGLISH GIRL:

I don't see why you keep having these morbid thoughts. Many soldiers return from wars unhurt, only to engage in some peaceful occupation in the pursuit of which they are killed by some unforeseeable accident.

MOTHER:

Oh!

ENGLISH GIRL:

Hugh is as safe in the army of General Cornwallis as he would be right back here at home. After all, General Washington's army is made up only of seedy criminals and starving bootblacks! They have neither food nor equipment, and everyone says it is not possible that they shall hold out for more than a few weeks against the skilled and well-equipped troops of our English army. In all probability the war has already ended in our favor, and but for the slow and sluggish meanders of the ships bringing the news, we should be cognizant of it this day, this very hour.

MOTHER:

Child, Artella, you are kind. But, dear, when a people fights for its freedom, even though its army be composed of little children bearing branches, that people will never stop until it has attained that freedom; so that it seems that, inevitably, that people will win, and Hugh, if he stay long enough, be, of necessity, wounded or killed. And that is why I weep—for my only son.

ENGLISH GIRL:

But, Mother! the Americans cannot possibly win—they have no supplies!

SCENE 4

The British camp at night. Complete darkness.

26

FIRST AMERICAN SOLDIER:
    Jim?

SECOND AMERICAN SOLDIER:
    Yes, Jack?

FIRST AMERICAN SOLDIER:
    Jim, are you there, Jim?

SECOND AMERICAN SOLDIER:
    Yes, Jack, I'm here, right here. What did you want, Jack?

FIRST AMERICAN SOLDIER:
    Have you got some tobacco?

SECOND AMERICAN SOLDIER:
    Yes. Here.

FIRST AMERICAN SOLDIER:
    Thanks, buddy. It sure tastes good.

SECOND AMERICAN SOLDIER:
    Isn't it delicious? I'm glad you like it.

FIRST AMERICAN SOLDIER:
    It really is good.

SECOND AMERICAN SOLDIER:
    I get a lot of satisfaction from hearing you say that. Why don't you take a little more so you'll have some for after the raid?

FIRST AMERICAN SOLDIER:
    Aw, I don't want to—

SECOND AMERICAN SOLDIER:
    No, go on, really, take it. I want you to have it.

FIRST AMERICAN SOLDIER:
    Well, if you insist.

SECOND AMERICAN SOLDIER:
    I do.

FIRST AMERICAN SOLDIER:
    Thanks, Jim. You're . . .

SECOND AMERICAN SOLDIER:
    Don't try to put it into words, Jack. Let's just forget it.

FIRST AMERICAN SOLDIER:
    No—I . . .

SERGEANT (*cockney accent*):
    Quiet up there! This is supposed to be a sneak raid.

GEORGE WASHINGTON:
    What's the trouble here, Sergeant?

SERGEANT (*cockney accent*):
    God save your Honor, hit's a couple of the men, Sir, 'as been talking more
    than what they ought to 'ave, and I was for putting them in line, Sir.

GEORGE WASHINGTON:
    How long have you been in this country, Sergeant?

SERGEANT:
    Two months, Sir. Not long. But I feel hit's as much me own country as if
    I'd been 'ere fifty years, your Lordship.

GEORGE WASHINGTON:
    You wouldn't be a spy, by any chance, would you, trying to tip the enemy
    off by making noise?

SERGEANT:
    Bless me, no, your Lordship, by all that's sacred and 'oly. I am but a poor
    soldier would do 'is best to make this a land for free men to live and trade in.

GEORGE WASHINGTON:
    Very good. Continue with your work.

FIRST AIDE TO GEORGE WASHINGTON:
General Washington?

GEORGE WASHINGTON:
Is that you, Fitzdaniel? Haven't I told you not to use my name?

FIRST AIDE TO GEORGE WASHINGTON:
Begging your Worship's pardon, Sir, but I think we may have come on something, Sir. Here are many heads, arms, and legs, and if it is not the English camp, I know not what it might be.

GEORGE WASHINGTON:
Excellent. Every man on his stomach. Get away with everything you can. Food is most important. Next, ammunition and clothing. Whatever you do, make no noise. Kill no man unless absolutely necessary. Is that understood?

ALL (*whisper*):
Yes, General Washington.

(*Sounds of crawling about and scuffling.*)

CORNWALLIS (*in his sleep*):
What's that? Ho!

FIRST AIDE TO GEORGE WASHINGTON:
What was that noise?

SECOND AIDE TO GEORGE WASHINGTON:
The voice had a familiar ring.

FIRST AIDE TO GEORGE WASHINGTON:
Yes! it was Cornwallis.

SECOND AIDE TO GEORGE WASHINGTON:
Where does the English general lie?

FIRST AIDE TO GEORGE WASHINGTON:
Near us, most likely, since we heard him so clearly.

SECOND AIDE TO GEORGE WASHINGTON:

Let's go into his tent. It is likely to be rich in booty!

THIRD BRITISH SOLDIER (*waking up; speaks with an Irish brogue*):

Ooo-ooooooh me! (*Pause.*) Agh, it's little sleep I can be gettin', what with
the cold wind blowin' against me head, and me all the time thinkin' of those
that are near and those that are far away. And I did imagine as I lay thinkin'
that I heard almost a rustlin', a kind of noise almost, as if the winds
themselves had come to bring some news into our Irish camp. It's a little air
I'll be needin', and out of my tent I'll be steppin' and lookin' at the fair face
of the moon with all her tiny stars.

FIRST AMERICAN SOLDIER:

What's this?

SECOND AMERICAN SOLDIER:

It's a Limey, Jack.

FIRST AMERICAN SOLDIER:

Shall we drop him?

SECOND AMERICAN SOLDIER:

The General said no.

FIRST AMERICAN SOLDIER:

Then what shall we do?

SECOND AMERICAN SOLDIER:

Wait, and listen.

THIRD BRITISH SOLDIER:

Ah, 'tis a fair dark night, and such as it would be wrong to sleep through.
There is beauty in the blackness of the sky, which bears not one tiny star.
'Twould be a fair night for a murder, and that's certain, for a man cannot see
his hand before his face, even though he hold it up. A man could jump on
another on a night such as this and sink a blade in his back without bein'
noticed so much as a puff of smoke on a cloudy day. It's glad I am that the camp
is guarded well by stalwart Irish soldiers and that we are safe from all harm.

SECOND AMERICAN SOLDIER:

Quick, into his tent!

FIRST AMERICAN SOLDIER:
> Supposing he comes back?

SECOND AMERICAN SOLDIER:
> Then we'll have to—

FIRST AMERICAN SOLDIER:
> No!

SECOND AMERICAN SOLDIER:
> Yes! But he may not come. Come on, Jack!

FIRST AMERICAN SOLDIER:
> Lead the way!

GEORGE WASHINGTON:
> Sergeant, tell the men that the object of the raid has been accomplished. We have more than enough supplies for the campaign. Have them re-assemble here, and we will then depart for our own camp.

SERGEANT:
> Yes, Sir. Yes, Sir. Oh, yes, Sir!

(Much crawling and scuffling.)

GEORGE WASHINGTON:
> Men, the raid has succeeded. We return to the American camp tonight!

ALL:
> Hurrah for General Washington!

SCENE 5

The English camp, next day.

CORNWALLIS (*running out of his tent*):
> Help! I've been robbed! My guns, my clothes, my food supplies—everything is gone!

FIRST AIDE TO CORNWALLIS:
> And so have I! Everything is gone, everything!

SECOND AIDE TO CORNWALLIS:
And I.

THIRD BRITISH SOLIDER (*Irish brogue*):
And I.

COOK:
The kitchen tent is completely emptied of supplies!

QUARTERMASTER:
All our equipment and ammunition are gone!

ASSISTANT QUARTERMASTER:
And our clothing!

FIRST AIDE TO CORNWALLIS:
What shall we do?

SECOND AIDE TO CORNWALLIS:
Who has done this deed? It is impossible—

CORNWALLIS (*suddenly enlightened; is his calm self once more*):
Men, return to your quarters. Do not be alarmed. I shall issue instructions for your further conduct. Demoda and Bilgent, come with me.

(*All leave, save for* CORNWALLIS *and his two* AIDES.)

FIRST AIDE TO CORNWALLIS:
If it please your Grace, how—?

SECOND AIDE TO CORNWALLIS:
If your Lordship knows—

CORNWALLIS:
Precisely. It is very simple. The man Washington has duped us. In the dead of night, he and his soldiers must have crept into our camp and stripped us of supplies. It is the only possibility. The man is a genius! If only we could win him over to our side . . . I've got it! Bilgent, you were once on the stage. Go to my tent. There is one trunk there they did not steal, because it was anchored to the ground. Take this key and open it. Inside you will find the uniform of an American officer. Put on this uniform and present yourself

to General Washington, saying you have been sent to him by General Stevens, in Haskell. Then, when you have won his confidence, convince him of the justness of our cause. Washington is a righteous man, and if he is convinced we are right he will join us without hesitation. The future of England may depend on your mission! Take this key, and go!

(FIRST AIDE TO CORNWALLIS *leaves.*)

Now, Demoda, we must figure out a plan to obtain supplies. Our rear section is only three hours' march away, and we can easily reach them and resupply ourselves unless one thing happens—unless Washington is able to cut us off; and that he can do in one way only, by crossing a river—I forget its name. At any rate, there is little danger of his doing so, for he and his men are probably asleep after their strenuous night. Let's organize and march!

SECOND AIDE TO CORNWALLIS:
   Aye, aye, General.

SCENE 6

The American camp. George Washington's tent.

GEORGE WASHINGTON (*sitting on his bed*):
   I am tired, and I need sleep. Good night, America.
   (*Lies down and sleeps.*)

(*A placard is now displayed, which reads*
   THE DREAM OF GEORGE WASHINGTON.
   Throughout the dream, GEORGE WASHINGTON *the man remains sleeping on his bed, and the part of* GEORGE WASHINGTON *is played by a child actor.*)

GEORGE WASHINGTON:
   Where's Daddy, Mommy?

MOTHER:
   He'll be here in just a little while, dear. He's bringing you a present for your birthday.

GEORGE WASHINGTON:

Oh, Mommy! A real present?

MOTHER:

Yes, and you must thank him for it and be nice to your Daddy, as he loves you very much. Here he is now!

(*Enter George Washington's* FATHER. *He is carrying a young cherry tree, which he gives to* GEORGE.)

FATHER:

George, little George! Happy birthday to my little son!

(GEORGE WASHINGTON *cries.*)

MOTHER:

Why, baby, what's the matter?

GEORGE WASHINGTON:

Oh, Mommy, you said it was so nice, but it's all dirty and covered with roots!

FATHER:

What's the mater with the little crybaby? Is he afraid of getting his hands dirty?

MOTHER:

Oh, Elbert, you promised! Be nice to the child. It is a little one yet.

FATHER:

Humph! He'll never amount to a hill of beans, I can guarantee you that. All right, Sister, give me back the cherry tree! I'll give it to some other kid in the neighborhood, one who's a real man!

GEORGE WASHINGTON:

Oh, Daddy, don't! Is it really a cherry tree?

FATHER:

Come on, let go of it!

34

MOTHER:

Let the child keep it, dear. He wants it. He was only frightened at first, because it was so dirty and covered with roots.

FATHER:

All right, all right, he can have it. But give it to me! You don't think it's going to grow in your hands, do you, you little squirt? These things have to be planted, you know.

MOTHER:

Elbert, don't be so sarcastic. George only wants to be sure that you will not give the tree to another child.

FATHER:

No, of course I won't! I got it to give to him, didn't I? I only said that about another boy because he acted like he didn't want it before, like it was something that was no good, something dirty.

MOTHER:

George, go with your Daddy and help him plant the tree.

GEORGE WASHINGTON:

Yes, Mommy.

(GEORGE WASHINGTON *and his* FATHER, *plant the cherry tree, and both leave. Then* GEORGE WASHINGTON *comes back with a little axe and chops down the tree. The tree is carried off-stage, and once again all three members of the family appear.*)

MOTHER:

Oh, I'm so sorry to hear about that! I wonder who could have chopped it down?

GEORGE WASHINGTON:

I did, Mother. I cannot tell a lie.

MOTHER:

Oh, my darling! (*Hugs him.*)

FATHER:

What? You chopped down the tree I slaved for, you little brat? I'm going to give you the beating of your life!

35

MOTHER:

> Elbert, please!

FATHER:

> I'm going to give you a thrashing such as the world has never seen before!

GEORGE WASHINGTON:

> I cannot tell a lie, but I can run! I can flee from injustice! The tree was mine, to chop down as I pleased!

FATHER:

> I'll give you such a beating . . . !

> (GEORGE WASHINGTON *runs off, his* FATHER *following him.* MOTHER *remains.* FATHER *returns.*)

FATHER:

> He foxed me. He swam across the river. It was the only way he could have done it. The ONLY WAY!

> (MOTHER *and* FATHER *vanish, as the "Dream" placard is removed.*)

GEORGE WASHINGTON (*waking up suddenly*):

> Father! you help me now! Quickly, assemble the men! We march at once for the Delaware River!

SCENE 7

A grayish-blue, flat area in front of the Delaware: the river cannot be seen. GEORGE WASHINGTON *enters at the head of his troops.*

FIRST AIDE TO GEORGE WASHINGTON:

> We have marched quickly, and we have marched well. But what is the General's plan?

SECOND AIDE TO GEORGE WASHINGTON:

> He has not confided it to me, but I have gathered from little things that he has said that it is to cross the Delaware and cut off Cornwallis' army in its search for supplies.

36

FIRST AIDE TO GEORGE WASHINGTON:

Washington is a genius! The army with supplies is the army that wins the war. Washington has planned everything just right. First our night raid, which took away all of their supplies; and now this forced march, to cut them off in their attempt to renew their supplies.

SECOND AIDE TO GEORGE WASHINGTON:

You speak well. Washington has planned our every step. See how nobly he marches at the head of our troops!

GEORGE WASHINGTON:

Halt! Here let us stop and dismount and prepare the boats.

(*Busy activity—dismounting, boat-building, etc. Enter* FIRST AIDE TO CORNWALLIS, *disguised as an American officer.*)

FIRST AIDE TO CORNWALLIS (*to* GEORGE WASHINGTON):

I come to you from General Haskell, Sir, who is hard pressed at Stevens. I mean Stevens, Stevens, Sir, Stevens who is hard-hask at pretzelled, hart had at Prexelled, Sir, General Stevens, Sir, hart-passed at Haxel—

GEORGE WASHINGTON:

Tenwillet, remove this man at once to the medical tent, and place him under armed guard. He seems dangerous.

SECOND AIDE TO GEORGE WASHINGTON:

Yes, your Worship.

FIRST AIDE TO CORNWALLIS (*being led away*):

The man is a genius! It is impossible to deceive him.

GEORGE WASHINGTON:

Fitzdaniel, what news is there of Cornwallis's army?

FIRST AIDE TO GEORGE WASHINGTON:

He advances quickly, Sir, but by crossing at once, Sir, we shall be ahead of him by half an hour.

GEORGE WASHINGTON:

Then let us go! For only if we go swiftly shall we have victory! And only victory is sweet! Come, men, battalions, uniforms, weapons, come, across the Delaware—we have nothing to fear but death, and we have America to win!

(*They go. Two* OLD MEN *enter. Both stare in the direction in which* GEORGE WASHINGTON *and his army have gone.*)

FIRST OLD MAN:
What do you see?

SECOND OLD MAN:
I am old, and I see nothing.

FIRST OLD MAN:
I hear something, as though the sound of splashing.

SECOND OLD MAN:
I hear nothing. My ears are dead things.

FIRST OLD MAN (*suddenly very excited*):
Why do I ask you what you hear and see, when now I hear and I see. Do you know what I hear and see?

SECOND OLD MAN:
No.

FIRST OLD MAN (*rapt*):
I see General George Washington crossing the Delaware, with all his troops and horsemen. I see him standing up in his boat, but I cannot make out the expression on his face. The men and horses on the other side of the river are shaking themselves free of water.

SECOND OLD MAN:
Go on! Do you see anything else?

FIRST OLD MAN:
No. Now everything is dark again.

SECOND OLD MAN:
What you saw was enough.

(*Cannons boom.*)

FIRST OLD MAN:
The American army has crossed the Delaware.

END

THE DEATH
OF SIR
BRIAN CAITSKILL

THE DEATH OF SIR BRIAN CAITSKILL *was first produced by the Medicine Show Theatre Ensemble, New York, in 1986, directed by Barbara Vann. A more recent production took place at Here, also in New York, in 1995, directed by John Michael Carley.*

SCENE 1.   WINCHESTER PALACE

MEDLOCK:

    I like Sir Brian Caitskill, but I would not
    trust him for a moment with my daughter, sir!

MAYBELL:

    Then let's away! While we stand talking here
    They are together in some private nook
    In Bethany, where no one herds them about!

MEDLOCK:

    Lead where you say. I follow.
                          Let's away!

SCENE 2.   A CHAMBER IN BETHANY

SIR BRIAN:

    Pamela, love like ours is loving us.
    No shadow haunts us. We live in the sun
    Of our affections. Give me a little kiss.

PAMELA:

    Sir Brian, your proposals take my breath away!
    But I suppose there's no harm in a kiss—
    I've often kissed my Nurse, and Daddy too
    When he would go a-hunting or to the Bourse,
    And Mommy when she was alive—oh, Mommy!
    No, no! it might not be approved by Mommy!

MOTHER (*imitated by* SIR BRIAN):
>   Kiss on!

PAMELA:
>   My mother's voice. Then here, Sir Brian, my lips.
>   They're yours to press against your own, mayhap.
>   Take them ere my suspicious father comes.

SIR BRIAN:
>   Smack!! This is pleasure, this is painless fun!
>   Oh let's again—the moment is too sweet!

MAYBELL:
>   Sir Brian!

SIR BRIAN:
>   What? Who calls without?
>   Sir Emmeret Maybell . . . and—

MEDLOCK:
>   You churl!

PAMELA:
>   My father!

MEDLOCK:
>   Sir Brian Caitskill, I challenge you to a duel,
>   Tomorrow morning at five on Himsley Field!

SIR BRIAN:
>   Sir, I accept! No pleasure's greater than to kill a man
>   Whom one instinctively dislikes. However
>   It pains me to deprive you of a father,
>   Dear innocent kissable Pamela.

MEDLOCK:
>   Stay your words,
>   Foul churl, or I shall challenge you again!

SIR BRIAN:
>   But to what end? Tomorrow, then, at five!

42

MEDLOCK:

    On Himsley Field!

SCENE 3.   A TAVERN.

HUGH JEFFRIES:

    They say Sir Brian Caitskill duels tomorrow
    The father of innocent Pamela on Himsley Field
    And that the duel's occasioned by a kiss!

PETER KNOTT:

    They say Lord Medlock must outpistol him,
    For he's the greatest shot in the duelling world.

HUGH JEFFRIES:

    Yet Brian's young!

PETER KNOTT:

                  But pleasure-mad! and Medlock
    Defends his daughter's honor! What defends Brian?

(*Enter* SIR BRIAN.)

SIR BRIAN:

    My life! Good morrow, Lords. I see ye ready
    To lay me out a corpse. Well, we shall see!
    Give me a gallon of stout—there's pleasure in't,
    And inspiration too.

HUGH JEFFRIES:

              This duel sits well
    With Brian! See what clarity's in his eyes!

PETER KNOTT:

    It is the ale sits well. I fear he's drunk
    And will not go tomorrow to the field!

SCENE 4.   HIMSLEY FIELD

MEDLOCK:

>What say, Sir Emmeret Maybell? is he come?
>What says the clock? is it not five? the churl!

(*Enter, at a distance,* SIR BRIAN, *dressed as* MOCTEZUMA.)

PAMELA:

>He comes, he comes, and radiant feathers dress him
>From head to foot! Attired, one would say,
>As Moctezuma, Lord of Aztec Ind,
>And such a gentleness sits on his brow!
>It were a crime to kill him!

MEDLOCK:

>   Silence, daughter!
>I only brought you here because you would
>Not stay at home. It is not proper that
>You be here.

PAMELA:

>   See you not how gaily dressed
>He is in fact, dear father?

MAYBELL:

>   She speaks truly,
>Lord Medlock; he like to an Indian prince
>Doth move across the field.

MEDLOCK:

>   Why, then I'll kill
>An Indian prince, so long as his same corpse
>Be found inside the feathers! Let's to guns!

(MEDLOCK *and* SIR BRIAN *fire.* BRIAN *falls.*)

SIR BRIAN:

>You have shot well. One word, Sir, ere I die,
>With your fair daughter?

MEDLOCK:

Speak, poor feathered ass!

PAMELA:

Father!

SIR BRIAN:

Pamela, listen, my life concludes
With many a harsh and vile discordant note,
But I could change all to a symphony
By whispering one moment in your ear.

(*He whispers.*)

PAMELA:

He said he loved me, sir, would marry me
If he were still alive. He found you harsh . . .

(SIR BRIAN *dies.*)

MEDLOCK:

He is dead!

MAYBELL:

He was a gallant duelist
And stood the gaff, though he came strangely to't!

MEDLOCK:

See that his body, dressed in all its pomp,
Is given fitting burial. We weep
That we have killed him.

(*Enter* GEORGE HENDERSON.)

GEORGE HENDERSON:

This your custom, sir,
Is by the much too rash—this duelling,
Which for a puff of pride, has taken here
An honest life, that wanted but a kiss!
It is unwarranted, and should be banned.

45

MEDLOCK:

    Sir, you are generous in disquisition,
    But here your counsel is unwanted.

GEORGE HENDERSON:

I

    Forbear to prophesy, but mark my words:
    This duel shall end duelling in England—
    And Brian Caitskill not have died in vain!

MEDLOCK:

    Come, trumpets, let's away!

END

THE
CONSTRUCTION
OF BOSTON

THE CONSTRUCTION OF BOSTON *was first produced at the Maidman Playhouse, New York, in May, 1962. The play was a collaboration with three artists—Niki de Saint-Phalle, Jean Tinguely, and Robert Rauschenberg, who did sets, costumes, and decor. Once the construction of a city was decided on as a subject, Rauschenberg chose to bring people and weather to Boston; Tinguely, architecture; and Niki de Saint-Phalle, art. The people Rauschenberg brought to Boston were a young man and woman who set up housekeeping on the right side of the stage. For weather, Rauschenberg furnished a rain machine. Tinguely rented a ton of gray sandstone bricks for the play, and from the time of his first appearance he was occupied with the task of wheeling in bricks and building a wall with them across the proscenium. By the end of the play the wall was seven feet high and completely hid the stage from the audience. Niki de Saint-Phalle brought art to Boston as follows: she entered, with three soldiers, from the audience, and once on stage shot a rifle at a white plaster copy of the Venus de Milo which caused it to bleed paint of different colors. A cannon was also fired but did not go off. Niki de Saint-Phalle and Tinguely had doubles who spoke or sang their lines; Rauschenberg's lines were not spoken at all but were projected, at the appropriate times, on a screen. The work was directed by Merce Cunningham; the music was by John Dooley. The Chorus was played by Richard Libertini and MacIntyre Dixon. In 1989 The Construction of Boston was made into an opera, with music by Scott Wheeler, and was presented, first, with the John Oliver Chorale, at the Old South Church in Boston, then, in a different production, in 1990, at the Charlestown Working Theatre, also in Boston.*

NOTE: *After the opening dialogue,* SAM *and* HENRY *become the* CHORUS *and as such speak for a number of different personae. In the Maidman Playhouse production the two speakers alternated frequently—at the beginning of speeches, when there was a break in the course of a long speech, and usually at the beginning and end of quoted passages inside speeches— such as, for example, the statement by Beacon Hill in the first* CHORUS *speech.*

The scene is modern Boston. Backdrop of Boston buildings.

HENRY:

Hello Sam.

SAM:

Hello Henry.
See where Boston stands so fair
And cruel. Have you ever thought
Once there was nothing there?

HENRY:

I never thought of that!
You mean there was mere space?
No Milk Street, S. S. Pierce, and no South End?
No place where the postman walks, no bend
To turn toward Needham, waiting for one's date
Or for one's fate, no building to sit in?

SAM:

Well—even more—before the first man came to pass
This site and called it "Boston," there was nothing—
Merely grass and sea: three high hills called Trimountain:
Beacon, Pemberton, Vernon,
And the salt sea—wallahhah!
And the Cove.

HENRY:

And were there nymphs
Inhabiting this grove?

And demigods, and other treasure-trove
Of ancient days?

SAM:

There were. They built this city.
Not ancient Botticelli
Nor sky-inspired Bellini
Ever trembled to
A sight more beautiful
Than Boston in her ancient days
And during her creation!
They say men came then who were more than men,
Who from one market reared a whole town up,
Made urban weather to give urban dreams,
Built high brick walls where once there flowed fresh streams.

HENRY:

Ah, fair to tell!

SAM:

Yet none were satisfied
Until one greater Spirit came, who changed
What they had done and made it beautiful.

HENRY:

What kind of Spirit?

SAM:

A woman—

HENRY:

Beautiful?

SAM:

Incredibly so—But

HENRY:

What is happening?

SAM:

But now I feel faint

50

HENRY:

Everything is growing dark

A VOICE:

You speak of one men are not fit to know;
Such knowledge is not fit for mortal tongue.
Therefore this darkness. All must come again
As it has come before. You have undone
Three hundred years of building by your chatter
Of sacred things. This darkness signifies
Your crime; and your purgation shall be this:
You must see Boston built again
Just as it was before—perhaps, though, faster.
Oh tremble, mortals! Now, let there be nothing
But grass, Trimountain, and the answering sea!

(*Total darkness.*)

(*Lights go on. Boston has vanished.*)

CHORUS:

How strange! What freshness steals across my brow!
Delightful breezes, song of twittering birds,
And the faint smell of grass mixed with the spray.
See where the hawthorn blossoms, and the rose!
Ah in this wilderness let me remain
Forever! Here man's heart and brain find peace!
The year is 1630, peaceful year!
How lovely it is here!
And even nature seems to sing in joy!
Huge Beacon Hill cries out in gusty tones,
"How happy I am now, fat as a cow
And higher than a treetop's loftiest bough—
I'm made of mud and gravel
And squirrels up and down me travel
Which gladly I allow."
The light blue summer day
Reflected in Back Bay (*Enter* RAUSCHENBERG.)
Shines like an eye—but stop—who comes here now?
Who is he? oh, what kind of man is he?

This seems to me no man, but more than man!
Hail, Populator. . . .
What shall you to this barren coastland do?

RAUSCHENBERG:

Bring people!
And manufacture weather for the people.

CHORUS:

He hopes to have a city here—
At least a little town—that's clear—
Or else why bring the people down?

RAUSCHENBERG:

That's clear. Here!

(RAUSCHENBERG *brings people*).

CHORUS:

He's bringing people.

RAUSCHENBERG:

And weather, too.

CHORUS:

There is already weather.

RAUSCHENBERG:

I'm bringing more. Cities need weather different from the country's.
Otherwise why would people go to the country? I'm bringing city weather
here. I need it for the city.

CHORUS:

Dark afternoons in autumn he
Brings to Boston peerlessly
And in winter with the hush
Of evening, miles of snow and slush!
Springtime warmth, exploding late,
Daisies 'mid the fish and freight;
Sultry summer afternoons
To make the Boston citizens
Dressed in high style, dressed to the tens,

Uncomfortable as baboons—
Oh where has our lovely climate gone?
Ah Rauschenberg, have mercy!
Yet it's lovely,
And seems just right for Boston, I'll admit.
I'd almost swear that I can hear
The weather speaking as he brings it here
To be a part of Boston—
There is a deep gruff voice: "I am the storm!
I have a lovely loud mellifluous form
When I'm alone. Ah, but in the city
Bumped against the fire escape,
Mailbox and wall, I lose my shape,
And lightning rods poke into me—
Oh let me be a storm at sea!"
"No, no," says Rauschenberg.
And now we hear the summer noon
Whose voice is rather like a croon:
"Ah in the country let me be!
Tall buildings are the death of me!
They block my light and make me black
And humid: sweat runs down my back!"
But Rauschenberg says, "Noon, march on."
And we hear the summer dawn
Complaining now to Rauschenberg:
"Bob, this transfer is absurd!
In the country redbirds sing
When they see me: everything
Cries aloud for joy! But here amid
The stench of fish and people
Black roadway and black steeple
What function can I serve? I like to please."

RAUSCHENBERG:

You shall, my tease,
My love, my delectation!
When you come
The city's heart shall, like a muffled drum,
Begin to beat, and as you go you'll see
Proffered to you constantly
Every single business day

A great urban-souled bouquet
Of people and their actions!

CHORUS:

That sounds fine! And now he brings divine
And holy moonlight, which says, "I
Am interrupted here," but Rauschenberg replies:
"So by your interruption shall you shine
More brilliantly and wake a million dreams
Instead of one: besides which, we need moonlight in the city."

RAUSCHENBERG:

And now I have to stock
The city up with people!

PEOPLE (*spoken by* CHORUS):

We are Irish, we're Italian,
We are British, why has he
Brought us here to stock this city
As if it were an aquarium,
As if we were human fish?

CHORUS:

Every city needs some people,
And a racial mixture functions
Very nicely in America.
You should be glad to be together—
Very exciting things will happen!
Ah I can hardly restrain myself
From singing praise to Rauschenberg
When I see this racial mixture!
How enthralling! How exciting!
And, in the harbor, fish are biting!

RAUSCHENBERG:

Now I think I've done—

CHORUS:

All hail, great Rauschenberg!

RAUSCHENBERG:

>   And yet there's only one

CHORUS:

>   All hail to you!

RAUSCHENBERG:

>   Thing wrong. We have the weather and the people,
>   But they, the people, have no way to get
>   Out of the weather or back into it.
>   We need some BUILDINGS!

CHORUS:

>   Tinguely, spirit of the air,
>   Now descend, and kill despair!
>   Aid us with your mighty hands
>   Molding earth to your commands!
>   O spirit, come!

>   (TINGUELY *appears.*)

TINGUELY:

>   I am
>   Arrivèd!
>   Ah! what a lovely layout you have here!
>   What varied weather and what varied people!
>   What lovely mountains and what snappy sea!
>   I'll do it, Rauschenberg, for it inspires me!
>   Oh it sends great create-
>   Ive tremors all though me!

CHORUS:

>   All hail to Tinguely! We need houses to live in.

TINGUELY:

>   Peace, citizens—that's where I'll begin,
>   Quite naturally.

CHORUS:

>   Tinguely, we need public buildings.

55

TINGUELY:

   Certainly! And ones with gildings—
   That's my next endeavor!

CHORUS:

   I have never
   Seen such immense intense inflamed construction!
   Oh like the beaver speeded at his work
   Is Tinguely the great architectural Turk!
   See how he functions! ah! ah!

TINGUELY:

   But now we need more space!
   How shall I solve this problem, tell,
   For now we need more space!
   Ha! Ha! I've got it! Now!

CHORUS:

   Help, help!
   My God, Tinguely, what are you doing? What are you trying to do? What
      are you going to do?

TINGUELY:

   The city needs more land area. Thus I am going to fill the Mill Pond with
   the top of Beacon Hill. Two, I am going to fill the Back Bay with sand, from
   Needham, Mass. Thirdly, I am going to extend Boston out into the harbor
   by means of docks.

CHORUS:

   O brave ambition!
   And see how he proceeds,
   Ah mighty Tinguely!
   Yet hear that cry
   From Beacon Hill, which rends the sky,
   "Oh do not dig me, Tinguely!
   Oh Tinguely, leave me be!"
   But he remorselessly
   Goes digging on; and now he fills the Pond,
   Which merely gasps, and now he smiles
   To see poor Beacon Hill reduced by miles,
   And now he turns another way

And contemplates the old Back Bay
And starts to fill it too.
At which the old Bay cries as to the skies:

"Boston, all that I can say
Is, it's grand to be a bay!
First you're full and then you're empty,
Then your friends go to the country—
They come back and fill you in:
All shall be as it has been.
Fill me up with sand and gravel,
No more boats across me travel—
And my chest where children play
Is black by night and brown by day.
Now I feel the sidewalks, clunk!
Slapping down on me, kerplunk!
And I feel the buildings rising
Filled with chairs and advertising
Where was once a boat capsizing,
Splashes, and a frightened brow—
There is nothing like that now!
Oh the buildings are so heavy—
How they weigh me down!"

Now you're the *town*,
Back Bay—you mustn't complain!
It's wonderful to be a part
Of an existent urban heart
Where on hot summer days
The heat sings its own praise
By sheer cement!

"I know that's true—
And I knew what you meant
Before you said it; still, my dear, do you
Know what it's like to feel upon your body
A seven-story home where there was only foam
Before? What used to be my shore
Ça ne l'est plus encore!"

TINGUELY:

>   Back Bay, you're lucky. You and Mill Pond are.
>   I am going to put
>   Sumptuous buildings on you that
>   Will make you lovely as a star.

CHORUS:

>   What? More?
>   What? More?

TINGUELY:

>   Come buildings, ah my airy darlings, come!

CHORUS:

>   They say he is a man, and yet he looks
>   Much like a woman to me. Yet he builds
>   Extremely like a man! They say his beard
>   Betrays his male identity, and yet—
>   And yet his skirt suggests he is a woman!
>   Perhaps this is an artist who combines
>   The sensitivity and strength of both
>   And is a whole man, such as Hesiod sung!
>   Oh man or woman, he can surely put
>   The buildings up! that noise of bumping fills
>   The atmosphere! and feel that weight upon us!

TINGUELY:

>   Now! now! I've done it! they are part of it!
>   Now to the seaside to fill in the sea!

CHORUS:

>   Fairest Tinguely, we the wharfs,
>   Splintery helpless wooden dwarfs,
>   Make appeal to you:
>   We love the water.
>   And if you'd be our friend, great building man,
>   O build us into her, thus let our natures
>   Sink down in her, oh let us fill the harbor
>   Till Boston's two times Boston's present size.

TINGUELY:

> Sweet wharfs, I'm glad to see you are in love;
> Your plan is just what I was thinking of.
> Yes it's exactly what I thought about—
> O bump bump bump throughout
> The cove and harbor spread you out
> Until we have a coastline that's in fact
> A kind of wood and water pact,
> A marriage of the forest to the sea!

CHORUS (*as water*):

> What do I feel sink into me?

CHORUS (*as wharfs*):

> It's only we, dear harbor—
> Oh sweetheart, sister, mother!

CHORUS (*as water*):

> O close-clutched ecstasy!

TINGUELY:

> Well, wharf and water seem well satisfied—
> I hope the city will be too. Now what have I to do
> But plant a few more buildings here
> And then rush back to Scollay Square
> And, after, glance about
> To see what things I have left out—
> Ah, Commonwealth Avenue!
> I must make you, and then I've finished!

CHORUS:

> See how the smiling city takes its shape:
> Fair Scollay shining like a stem of grape;
> And Beacon Hill, though cut into,
> Still like an orange to the view
> Of one who sees it from Longfellow Bridge!
> O Tinguely, Rauschenberg, it's fine
> And yet I can't help feeling
> Something sublime is gone: pure nature—roses; sparrows singing;
> > redbird; bluejay; twit-twit-twitter-twee!
> It seems such a short time ago we had that here!

Oh tell me, how can we get back what's gone?
I miss the fresh air and the lovely feeling!

RAUSCHENBERG:

Don't you like cities? It's
A fine time to ask me,
A fine time to bring *that* up!
Why Tinguely is already underground
                             (*thump thump*)
Building the subway, and you ask me how
To get back bubbling brooks?

CHORUS:

You don't know how?

                             (*Enter* NIKI.)

NIKI (*she sings*):

Well, I know how!
What this town needs is beauty, what Boston needs is art!
Let every heart rejoice,
Rejoice in every part
Of Boston!

                 (TINGUELY *emerges from the subway.*)

TINGUELY:

Well, the subway is finished!

NIKI:

But Boston is not quite.

CHORUS:

Men say she has a magic pistol
Which can turn plain glass to crystal
And can change an apple cart
To a splintery work of art!
Shooting at a person she
Makes him a celebrity!
Everything she does
Is not what it was—

60

Niki, bring us beauty's virtue!
Fire at that ancient statue—
Perhaps it has retained some value.

NIKI:

Here are streams—there are flowers
For the Public Garden's bowers! Let the flowers fall!

CHORUS:

O Niki de Saint-Phalle!
We knew that Boston could be beautiful,
But it was not until you came along.
Where were you, fairest of them all?

NIKI (*sings*):

Busy in Rome and Istanbul,
In Florence and in Paris;
Shooting landscapes in Shanghai
And portraits in Pekin;
Shooting rainbows in the sky,
Shooting the mosaics in
Saint Apollinaris.
I bring beauty and detail
By the shots which cannot fail
To delight the nation.
I make ugly statues fall,
And I give the palace wall
Lovely rustication.
I put features on the face
That is much too solemn;
I give a Corinthian grace
To the Doric column.
Why should I do anything
But be glad to make you sing
Praises to my shooting?
In my hand I have a gun,
And it is the only one
That gives columns fluting!
It's the only pistol which
Makes an empty canvas twitch
And become a painting!

It's the only gun that fires
Answers to the soul's desires—

CHORUS (*sings*):
Ah you are so pretty!

NIKI (*sings*):
Therefore on this summer night,
Citizens, for your delight,
I'll shoot up your city!

CHORUS (*sings*):
She'll shoot up the city.
(*Speaks:*)
There she goes!
From the top of old Beacon to the muddy Back Bay
There's a mumble of pleasure on this sunny day
As the shooting is heard to resound boom boom—
As the shooting is heard, like the cry of a bird,
And it's covering old Boston ground
With love and pleasure.
Well, has she finished?

NIKI:
Yes.
And now, at last, my time is past, I must be drifting homeward—
I go to treat art's plaster cast, both Parisward and Romeward!
Farewell, delicious citizens brought here
By Rauschen—Rauschen—what's his name? And dear
Great heavy streets of Tinguely, oh farewell!

CHORUS:
Now she drifts out to sea like a great bell!
How grand she is and fair!
We who feel our new creation
Run through us like syncopation
In the arms and tail
Praise her without fail!
Oh love which makes us new—
Newer than Rauschen—what's his name?—
Oh Niki, love for you,

It is which makes us new!
And like a nightmare which does not come true
This Boston now, which seems so old, is new
As if we saw the place for the first time
From the sublimest view-
Point: Mystic River Bridge—
And here is what we see, and it is beautiful,
Niki de Saint-Phalle, all because of you:
You have shot Boston full of love for you!
Ah, see how fair—
The outsize obelisk of Bunker Hill!

All hail to Tinguely for this masterpiece!
Below, on the left, the Boston Naval Shipyard,
Where Rauschenberg's creations slip
Beneath hot summer days he's given them
Up and down riggings of a full-rigged ship!
What sight so fair
As in this air
A seacoast made of ships!
To Rauschenberg then praise!
And there North Station, Beacon Hill,
Public Garden, swan with bill,
Restaurants where eat their fill
Fishermen and salesmen!
Here is Boston Latin tall,
There majestic Fanueil Hall,
Here's the Charles, and there's the Mall
And the Charles River Basin!
Who can count its beauties wholly?
Let us summarize them solely
Lest our praise proceed too slowly,
Niki dear, to you!

(TINGUELY *and* RAUSCHENBERG *kneel to* NIKI.)

TINGUELY:

Niki, all this city's buildings
With their warm old-fashioned gildings
I dedicate to you.

RAUSCHENBERG:

    Niki, all these sunlit people
    Or in shadow of a steeple
    I consign to you.

NIKI:

    And yet without you two, what could I do?
    We must have people and they have to live
    Inside of something: therefore I shall praise
    You equally, for fashioning this maze!
    For I cannot exist without the rest
    Of life, although I am perhaps what's best.
    Now, citizens, sunset cover you
    Oh fairest sunset cover you
    Now fairest Boston mother you and cover you and smother you, fair
        Boston cover you,
    (*Sings:*)
    And until then, ADIEU!

END

THE
RED
ROBINS

To Don, Kate, and Vanessa

THE RED ROBINS *was first produced at Guild Hall in East Hampton, New York, in August, 1977; then, in a more ambitious production, in New York City, at St. Clement's Theatre in January, 1978. Don Sanders directed and Vanessa James designed the costumes. Kyle Morris did the sets for East Hampton. For the New York production the sets were by a variety of artists: Jane Freilicher, Red Grooms, Vanessa James, Alex Katz, Katherine Koch, Roy Lichtenstein, and Rory McEwen. The New York City cast included Lynn Bowman, Kate Farrell, Steven Hall, Chris Hawthorne, Ken Kirschenbaum, James Lytras, and Martin Maniak as Red Robins; Don Schrader as the President, Christophe DeMenil as the Bird, Don Sanders as Santa Claus, Brian Glover as the Easter Bunny, and Taylor Mead as Mike the Tiger, Ni Shu, Jill's father, Terrence, and the Captain. The lighting was by Alan Adelman and the choreography by Wendy Biller.*

DRAMATIS PERSONAE

THE RED ROBINS, *a group of young pilots, each with his or her own airplane. They have come to Asia in search of excitement and adventure:* BOB, JILL, BILL, JIM, LYN, LOUIS, BUD.

SANTA CLAUS, *a powerful middle-aged man who is now a sort of leader of the* RED ROBINS. *Some things about his appearance suggest he is the traditional Christmas figure, others that he is not.*

THE EASTER BUNNY, *also middle-aged, the powerful enemy of* SANTA CLAUS *and the* RED ROBINS. *His traditional holiday identity is as ambiguous as that of* SANTA CLAUS.

THE PRESIDENT (*of the United States*), *middle-aged, appears in two guises—as the Good President and as the Bad President.*

AIDE *to the* PRESIDENT

THE MAN IN THE YELLOW COAT, *a retired Western diplomat living in Shanghai and devoting his life to philosophy.*

JILL'S FATHER *and* JILL'S MOTHER, *a middle-aged couple from Minneapolis.*

CAPTAIN (*of a ship*)

MEINHEER PUSHNER, *an old, retired Dutch-Irish Colonial official who is spending the last days of his life on a small tropical island.*

FIRST *and* SECOND NATIVE BEARERS

NI SHU, *an old and very celebrated Chinese philosopher.*

MOTHER *and* CHILD, *characters in* JILL'*s dream and residents of Tin Fan.*

MARIAN, *an island girl, a love slave.*

MIKE THE TIGER, *a man-eating tiger.*

THE SLIMY GREEN THINGS

DOG

OCTOPUS

TERRENCE, *a treacherous ape.*

FIRST *and* SECOND APE, *political leaders of L'Isola non Trovata.*

BIRD, *a mysterious talking bird.*

THE STARS

JIM THE PLANT

PYOTOR, *a gland.*

ROUGHIE, *a stone.*

ELIA, *a possibility.*

Also, WAITER, APES, MONKS, SHARDS, COLD BACHELORS, *others.*

ACT ONE

SCENE 1. *The springtime morning sky above Asia.*
Birdsongs. Then the sound of airplanes.
The RED ROBINS *appear in their planes.*

BOB:

Jill, that's the place, I think—look over there!
Mount Kin-to-pang! Those rocky, snowy slopes
Lead down to Inner Malay, where we're going
To hunt man-eating tigers.

JILL:

Yes! I see it.

BOB:

And after that, we'll go to Ching Tang Palace
Where we will get the Map That Shows All Rivers,
Including the Five Rivers of the Air—

BOB:

Look, up ahead—

JIM:

It's—Occhu Bocchu, Aplaganda Lake,
That celebrated haunt of octopus!
And, through that mist beyond those plains, Shanghai,
The City of Golden Stairways!

69

LYN:

> I can't see it.

LOUIS:

> It's still in mist. We should start going down.
> The Hindu monastery where I stayed
> Two years, just flashed beneath us, on the left.
> I think that's Tiger Jungle five miles off.

BUD:

> You're right. Bob, do you want to lead us in?

BOB:

> Yes! Jill, stay here beside me. Bud, go back
> And steady our formation from the rear.
> Apprise us of all dangers. Let's descend!

BILL:

> We'll follow you.

SCENE 2. *A Plateau in Malaya,*
where the RED ROBINS *have landed.*
They are all there, except for BOB, *who enters.*

BOB:

> Bill, get the guns! Let's go! I heard the tiger!

JILL:

> I think we really ought to wait some more.
> He said that he was coming.

BILL:

> We should wait.

BUD:

> We did receive the message yesterday
> That, after such long time, he'd meet us here
> And make the hunt with us.

70

BOB:

He's late!

JILL:

He'll come!

LYN:

If he said he would meet us here, he will.

JIM:

Well, I don't know! Some one of us could stay here
To meet him, wait for him, the rest go on . . .

BILL:

I gladly would.

BOB:

Well . . .

(*Sounds of a plane crashing. Enter* SANTA CLAUS, *a bit staggered at first. He has just made a crash landing.*)

BOB:

Well, no one has to stay to meet him now!

JIM (*To* SANTA CLAUS):

How good it is to have you back with us!
How are you? Are you well? We have been wondering.
We haven't been together since November!

SANTA CLAUS:

Had a hard landing! Robins! My sweet friends!
My bunch! My sweet collaborators, all,
In the adventures of the human heart!
God, but it's good to see you! I have been
Away so long, not out of choice, my friends,
But trapped in battle with that monstrous fiend
Who hates us, who brings shivers of revulsion
To all who care for life, that vile debris
Whose name you know so well.

BOB:

Battling with . . . HIM?

SANTA CLAUS:

The EASTER BUNNY! Yes, that mass of horror!
I thought him dead, at last—I had him caught
Inside the stony mass of Mount Kabongo,
But he punched his way out and followed me
Without my knowing, through the Burmese sky.
Just now he almost killed me, hit my plane
With fighter bullets strong as bolts of lightning!
But I hit his as well, and left him burning,
Unable to go on.

JILL:

Why does he hate us?

SANTA:

I've never known, but have supposed that he
Is jealous of my holiday celebrity—
Greater, he knows, than his. And then, again,
He envies our Red Robin happiness.
He is morose, alone.

BILL:

Could something cure him?

SANTA:

Perhaps. But perhaps not. In any case,
I think that he will cause us no more trouble,
Not for a long, long while. Of this enough,
Of him enough. I come to bring good news.
You got the letter that I sent you? Good.
Well, there is something else. Within a twelvemonth
The airways will be clear, and we'll be able
To try to reach that place, to fly, and land there,
Which we have so far scarcely dared to speak of
It seemed so out of reach—And, if we can . . .

LYN: (*Excited*)
You mean—do you mean—can it be—

SANTA CLAUS:

> TIN FAN!   *(A gong sounds.)*
> Yes, we perhaps at last may see Tin Fan,
> The legendary city of the East
> Where there is perfect happiness—TIN FAN!

(Another gong. SANTA CLAUS *pauses for a moment.)*

> But now, let's to the jungle, and the heat
> Of hunting tigers! We have vowed we would,
> A long time past, come help the Malays kill
> The great man-eater, bane of all their lives!

(They go off.)

SCENE 3.   *Jungle, Enter* BILL.

BILL:

> I've tried it, but I can't. This hunting no.
> I'd hunt for anything, but not to kill,
> Not kill what never had done harm to me.
> I know this Malay beast has eaten men,
> But I don't think it's fair that twenty people
> Should follow him with guns. I'd gladly stand
> Against him one to one. But I can't hunt him.

(A thrashing sound in the brush. BILL *turns about, thinking it is the* TIGER, *and aims his rifle. But it is* LYN.)

LYN:

> Bill! I am not the tiger! Listen! Listen!
> I think they've found him. How are you? I wondered—

BILL:

> There are no tigers any more. No tigers.
> I hate this hunt. I wish that it would end.

LYN:

> I'll stay with you.

BILL (*much happier now*):
> Intoxicating friend!
> Say why we should kill tigers, or they us?
> Let love be all, be our sole blunderbuss!

(BILL *embraces* LYN, *then they walk off.* BOB *enters, holding* MIKE THE TIGER *by the tail.*)

BOB:
> I've got the tiger, caught him by the tail,
> And now, by God, we'll find a way to shoot him!
> Robins, help!

(MIKE *escapes. Enter* SANTA CLAUS, BUD, JILL, JIM, *and* LYN.)

BOB:
> I had the tiger, but he got away!

SANTA CLAUS:
> We'll find him!

BUD:
> Damn! (*All run off. Re-enter* MIKE THE TIGER.)

MIKE:
> My name is Mike, and I am a man-eating tiger. My kind stems from up around Kuannon, which is an old Indian word for "ring-face," and I guess that region must have gotten its name from us tigers who wear upon our brownish-red faces one and sometimes two or three medium-sized white rings. Sometimes, when the harvest is good and the sheep are fat, I like to pounce down into the valley and carry off some plump little lambs to my den and eat them. But whether the harvest is good or not, my favorite food is men. Men have a *je ne sais quoi*, I guess you could almost say it was an "intellectual" flavor, that kind of flavor you can only develop after you have spent a few years engaged in speculative thought. It's like the patina on some of the beautiful Chinese jars that some of these men have made. It's an "extra." As we tigers say, "Man is the only animal who is his own sauce." I don't blame them for trying to kill us! How would you like to have somebody after you who wanted to eat you?

(*Enter* JIM THE PLANT.)

74

JIM THE PLANT:

> I am a tropical plant. My name, for you, is Jim. I have a more
> complicated name in plant language, a language which is completely
> unnoticed not to say undeciphered and which, even if it were discovered,
> would make the decipherment of Linear-B seem like child's play. At any
> rate, to continue. Now, I like tigers because tigers don't like plants. There
> are two ways of liking, obviously enough. I don't like to eat tigers or,
> really, to do anything with them, but I like the fact that they don't want to
> do anything to me. Do you like me? If so, which way do you like me of the
> two ways I have named?

(*Enter* PYOTOR, *a* GLAND.)

PYOTOR:

> I am a gland, a part of a red bird's body. Without me the bird would not
> function normally but would flap wildly around on one wing, screaming
> its head off. In fact, it is doing that now, because I am not "doing my
> part" but am, instead, talking to you. My name is Pyotor (in gland
> language), I live in the jungle inside this bird, and I am the organ which
> gives him his sense of balance and his ability to control his actions.

(*Enter* ROUGHIE, *a* STONE.)

ROUGHIE:

> My name is Roughie and I am a stone. You have walked over me many
> times and not noticed me. I don't blame you at all. But when you need a
> stone, to crush a rattlesnake or an asp, then, then you run through the
> jungle shouting, "Where is Roughie? Oh where is a stone? I'd give
> anything to find a stone!" Why don't you stop to appreciate me now?

(*Enter* ELIA, *an* AS–YET–UNDISCOVERED POSSIBILITY.)

ELIA:

> My name is Elia. I am a possibility which has not yet been discovered by
> mankind or by animals. I am ignorant. I don't even know whether I am a
> solid, a liquid, or a gas, an idea or an emotion. I am motionless. The
> rattlesnake moves right through me, and the Tibetan monkey-bear. Yes,
> you are right, I do know about other things, but I know nothing about
> myself. Please find me. I will love you if you do—if I am capable of that.

(*Darkness. All leave.*)

SCENE 4. *A Malay hospital room.* JIM *and* BILL *are there, and* LYN, *who is in bed, sleeping, feverish. She wakes up.*

LYN:

Oh! ah! what? Help! Gland! Roughie! Jim! What?
Tiger . . .

JIM (*leans over her*):

Lyn, Lyn, you have had a bad dream and that is all!
Wake up! Wake up! There was no tiger hunt!

BILL:

But, Jim—there was!

JIM:

Better to let her feel
That she was only dreaming, that it all
Was nothing but a nightmare. She is ill.
She needs to rest and sleep.

BILL:

Well, I'll away
To other precincts on this woeful day!

(BILL *leaves.*)

LYN (*to* JIM):

But—but, was it all a dream? I saw the tiger
And HEARD HIM SPEAK. That was the worst of all.
Do tigers speak? And then a redbird's body
Or part of it, a gland. And there was Roughie
A stone, and something unknown, named Elia . . .

JIM:

You know, the jungle
Is full of things that almost speak to us—
Not ever, really. Now, it's best you sleep
To get rid of the fever. When you're stronger
Perhaps we two can puzzle all this out.
I'll stay here while you're sleeping.

LYN:

Well, goodnight!

(LYN *sleeps.*)

JIM:

Strange that back in America I was,
True, a good student, but mostly interested
In engineering and other applied science.
That got me interested one day in airplanes
From the mechanical aspect of the thing.
Once I discovered them, I hardly slept
But kept on working at them day and night,
Tinkering with their engines and their wings.
And there seemed to come to me in the night
Visions of a surprising kind in which
My body was an airplane, or my spirit,
Whatever it is we think of as the soul,
And that it flew me anywhere I wished.
I met, that year, two people, Bob and Jill,
Who seemed to me some way the way I was.
They both loved airplanes. Jill liked poetry
And got me interested in that. They spoke
Of Asia as a place where we might find
Some consummation, some amazing answer
To everything, by what we'd see and do—
It made no sense to go there—but we went!
Soon there were more and we became a group
And called ourselves Red Robins. And we stayed.
And I met Lyn, who's lying here asleep,
Dreaming of roses now, I hope, not tigers
And frightful things from those unconscious depths
Which plague us humans all our lives whenever
Some little disk has slipped inside our minds.
Yes, I met Lyn. And also there began
A curious revolution of my spirit
Which made me less and less an engineer
And more and more a poet. I began
To write! and, writing, felt I had discovered
The secret motions of the soul and body
Which were, precisely, those my self became

When I went flying, nightly, in my dreams.
These poems, they seem hardly a natural thing,
Surely not natural they should seem so strange,
So necessary, and so immanent—
They are just notes on paper, after all!
And yet to me they seem more permanent,
Inspiring proof of happiness than all
The mountainous sides of Asia's God-hewn summits
Which leave us gasping on their slopes. Well, each
Is part of what I feel and know we are . . .
(*Turning to* LYN.)
Sleep soundly. I shall come to thee anon.

(*Now* JIM *sits down at a table and writes. Enter* SANTA CLAUS *and* JILL. *Their words are what he is writing.*)

SANTA CLAUS:
The love I feel for you, Jill, is so deep
That I can scarcely understand its force.
I thought you were too young for me. I thought
That thirty years made differences too steep
For hearts to cross, but I see I was wrong.

JILL:
Whenever I awake, or when I sleep,
When silent, or when busy with discourse,
When sitting, lying, walking, I am caught
By feelings of a sort I cannot keep
From speaking of to you, they are so strong.
You know—I love you!

SANTA CLAUS:
You love me, too?
Fade, Mount Kabongo, in your circling mist!
Fade, house! Fade, palm trees! Fade, all I have known
Up to this moment, sacreder to me
Than gold to misers, pollen to the bee,
Or Asia to us all!

(*They embrace, then leave.*)

78

JIM (*looking up from his writing*):

 I'll finish it later. So far it's pretty good,
 It seems to me a sort of play in poetry.
 There is another part I have in mind
 About an island and a war with apes.
 She's waking up!

LYN:

 Well, I feel better.

(SANTA CLAUS *runs in.*)

SANTA CLAUS:

 Hurry! Lyn, are you better? Ah, I'm glad!
 If so, let's hurry! There is news that we
 May soon have dealings with the President
 Of the United States!

JIM:

       How can that be?
 What's he to do with us, or we with him?

SANTA CLAUS:

 I don't know, but he's coming.

LYN:

        Oh how strong
 This feeling is, that I approach my fate
 And never can escape it!

(JIM *sees her consternation and goes over and embraces her. She trembles.*)

JIM:

      My sweet love!

  S C E N E 5 . *The White House. A private chamber.*
 The PRESIDENT *sits at his desk, re-reading a letter he has written.*

PRESIDENT:

 "Dear Lyn . . ." I wonder if she'll believe I'm writing

79

To ask her for her hand. No, it's too ridiculous.
I love her, but it's crazy. I'll tear this up!

(*He tears up the letter and then sets fire to it. Smoke. Enter, in haste, a White House servant—he is really the Red Robin,* BUD, *in disguise.*)

BUD (*affecting a German accent*):
    Sir, Sir, vot is de trouble here? Vere from de smoke?

PRESIDENT:
    Oh, it's nothing. A letter I was writing.
    Here, young man, take these ashes off for me.

BUD:
    Dot I vill.

PRESIDENT:
    Thanks much.

(*He goes out.*)

BUD (*dropping the German accent and revealing his true identity*):
    . . . And will
    Survey their contents for I much suspect
    (I am Bud, Red Robin of a long renown)
    They have some matter relevant to us . . .
    Ha! Here's the burned name "Lyn." "I love you"—What?
    Our President loves Lyn? How curious!
    He is a man I thought was too important
    To care about such things. I'll take this letter
    To Santa Claus. Away!

(BUD *rushes off.*)

PRESIDENT (*re-enters*):
    Curse! damn, damn, curse! that she's so young and I so eminent!
    O would I were a worm upon the ground
    Of foul Tibet, that I might touch her foot! Alas, no help!
    My words rise up, but I remain below.
    We Presidents were ever fettered so!

SCENE 6.   *An airfield, on a plateau.* BUD *runs to* SANTA CLAUS
with the letter.

SANTA CLAUS (*reading it*):
> Thank goodness you got there in time!
> Ho! everybody! The President isn't coming after all!

BUD:
> Let us away, then, to Shanghai.

SANTA CLAUS:
> Good!
> I'll go there first to make sure all is safe.

SCENE 7.   *A Party, on a dark night in the Jungle.*
All the RED ROBINS *are there except for* BOB.
Some are dancing. The atmosphere is hushed and romantic.
Enter in a great hurry, BOB, *in goggles and helmet, ready to fly.*

BOB:
> Come on, everybody! We've got to pack up our airplanes and go!

BILL:
> What great incentive moves you on this night,
> When we are all so gay at this mild party,
> Friend Bob, to urge us to such sudden action?
> Have all the apes got ready to attack?
> Are octopus about to suck us down
> Into the very bosom of the deep?
> What is the reason for this hurry, friend?

BOB:
> It's time to go to Shanghai. It is the time
> When we must go. It is the ideal time
> When morning's sunshine mirrored on the stairways
> Can show another sky. It is the time
> When Shanghai's mist has cleared and is the time
> To fly there, and to be there, and to see.
> Red Man has sent me word.

BILL:

I should have thought
That you would rather stay here now, with Jill.

BOB:

It's not that way. Jill's feelings are her own,
And whom she loves, she loves. It is not me.

JILL:

Oh, Bob. Dear Bob! I've loved you, I feel something. I don't know.
I feel, for Santa Claus, some other thing
Quite past control—a sort of exaltation . . .

BILL:

So, upward! To the Stairways of Shanghai!

(*All leave quickly, to get in the planes.*)

SCENE 8. *The streets of Shanghai, with strange, beautiful unattached stairways. Enter* SANTA CLAUS, *who climbs up one of the stairways. Enter* LYN *and* BILL, *who walk about looking at the city.* BILL *sees* SANTA CLAUS.

BILL:

Santa Claus—greetings! Glad you came here first.
How is the city? Safe? All as we hoped?

SANTA CLAUS:

Yes, safe. We've come here in a time of peace.
And we are protected by a group of monks
Whose leader is Louis, on the Southern Wall
Which is the only place some crazy foe
Could even try to enter. The Easter Bunny,
I think, though, will not dare attack us here.
Ah, these old stairways! They are beautiful
Like nothing else on earth—some made of glass,
Some made of thinnest paper, some of gold,
Others of rubies and of emeralds!
Free-standing stairways for five thousand years
Have multiplied in Shanghai, until, now,
No matter where one stands, on King Ching Street

82

Or at the Pong Chai Gate, one's thoughts are upwards,
As surely as one's eyes, in strangest ways.
Well, walk, see what you can. We'll reassemble
And speak some hours later. I must go
Elsewhere in Shanghai for a while. Goodbye!

(SANTA CLAUS *leaves.*)

BILL:

> The stairways of Shanghai! (BILL *sees* LYN.) Lyn! Look at them!
> Let's climb one—would you like to?

LYN:

> Let me see.
> I have a guide to Shanghai. Let's begin
> With here, this one, the Ho Ka Palisade.
> This is the "Paper Stairway of the Gods."
> Pity the man who set a match to this!

BILL:

> For the gods would destroy him.

LYN:

> I believe
> They are entirely colored gold and silver.
> Look at them in the noontime. How they gleam!

(*They start to climb the gold and silver stairway.*)

BILL:

> Wait! what? Lyn, stop! oh, listen! I heard something,
> Some sounds as if of shouting down below.

(*Enter, agitatedly, some Buddhist* MONKS.)

MONKS:

> Ha ha ho! They have captured Louis! Help!
> They have entered into the city and may doom
> All the Red Robins who are on the stairs.
> Where's Santa Claus? There's Bill and Lyn there—ho!

LYN:

    What—?

BILL:

    Don't be afraid!

(LYN *and* BILL *run down stairs to the street. Re-enter* SANTA CLAUS.)

SANTA CLAUS:

    What's this? Got in? Well, so—
    The SLIMY GREEN THINGS are the only answer!

LYN:

    What are the slimy green things?

BILL:

                 What are they?

SANTA CLAUS:

    That Santa Claus commends them? You shall see!

(*Enter* BOB, *then* JILL.)

BILL:

    What's up?

SANTA CLAUS:

             I'm going to call the Slimy Greens!

JILL:

    Good God, dear Santa, do it carefully!

(*Enter,* BUD.)

BUD:

    There's not much time.
    The Southern walls are all aswarm with enemies.
    I've just come from there. Neal and I were on
    The Chi Chung Escalier and saw them swarming!

SANTA CLAUS:
>What are their names?

BUD:
>>Don't know. Cold Bachelors, mostly!
>I recognized a few of them, I think.
>Behind them rose a great white pair of ears
>And there was bunny sniffing.

SANTA CLAUS:
>>That I knew.
>Well, we must find the Slimies. Let's fan out—
>Bud you to east, Jill west, I to the south
>Where most the danger is, Jim you to north
>And with you Lyn and Bill—there in the north
>Is where I think the Slimy Green Things are—

JILL:
>How will we recognize them when we find them?

SANTA CLAUS:
>Oh you'll know when you find them! (SANTA CLAUS *gives all the* RED
>>ROBINS *some seeds.*) When you do,
>Scatter this seed where you would have them follow.
>Don't worry. They won't harm you. They are gentle.

BILL:
>How will they help us in our fight?

SANTA CLAUS:
>>They have
>A special poison gas which they exude
>When they are close to rabbits. I've a mask
>Which will protect me, but you should stay back
>When they come near our foes. I'll hold them back
>Until you get there with the Slimy Green Things.
>Hurry, though! I cannot hold out too long!

(*All go off.*)

SCENE 9. *A beautiful city garden in Shanghai.*
LYN *wanders in, looking for the* SLIMY GREEN THINGS.
She is intrigued by the beauty of the garden.
The MAN IN THE YELLOW COAT *comes in absorbed*
in his thoughts; he is holding a cigar.
LYN *hides behind a tree.*)

MAN IN THE YELLOW COAT:

And what is the answer? what can it mean that we are born into paradise
or nothingness? and that we spend our earliest years in paradise or
nothingness, though subject to pain, and that when we are twelve or
thirteen we seem to be lifted into another sphere (a stratosphere or
sexisphere) of paradise or nothingness. We are always filled with
excitement over life as well as with the ignorance of all that it means—
beset by passion, not knowing if we are loving a ghost, beset, beset . . .

LYN (*appearing to him*):

There were so many blue wasps that summer! so many young girls
dancing in frocks at the hotel! so much orange! so many teeter-totters left
abandoned in the public square!

MAN IN THE YELLOW COAT:

What? Who are you? What?

LYN:

The railroad train stopped. It looked like a smokestack.
Then green spots started to appear all over its wheels
and sides.

MAN IN THE YELLOW COAT:

Lyn, you must find the ring!

LYN:

What ring?

MAN IN THE YELLOW COAT:

The Ring of Destiny! Yes, for with that ring, and only with it, you will be
able to get to Tin Fan—the Country of Desire Fulfilled!

LYN:

Oh! And the Slimy Green Things? I have to find those now.

86

MAN IN THE YELLOW COAT:

They are just ahead of you a little ways.

LYN:

And the ring?

MAN IN THE YELLOW COAT:

I can't tell you any more about that.

(LYN *goes off left, where there is an increasing green glow. It is the Slimy Green Things. The* MAN IN THE YELLOW COAT *starts off right.*)

LYN:

The Green Things are here! But what on earth can that mean about the "ring"?

MAN IN THE YELLOW COAT:

I must phone the President!

SCENE 10. *Shanghai—the Southern Gate and the Chi Chung Escalier.*
Enter EASTER BUNNY *and* COLD BACHELORS (*his henchmen*).

EASTER BUNNY:

Come! come! They are defeated. They cannot resist us any further.
Come! come! They are defeated! Come away, come!

FIRST COLD BACHELOR:

Master, one stands beyond and challenges
Your mighty self to come do combat with him.
He says his name is one that you well know.

EASTER BUNNY:

Were he the greatest bully on this earth
I should not fear him.

FIRST COLD BACHELOR:

He is dressed in red,
Has a white beard and very savage smile.

EASTER BUNNY:

> At last, that monster Claus. Give me my armour.
> Let these white limbs in steel be buckled up
> And I shall go against this worst of evils!

(*He arms himself.* SANTA CLAUS *appears.*)

EASTER BUNNY (*to the* COLD BACHELORS):

> Stay here close hidden. If the advantage turns
> To that same bearded fool, take aim and kill him.
> I do not plan to toy with life this day.
> He'll die, no matter what.

FIRST COLD BACHELOR:

> Yes, Master, yes.

EASTER BUNNY:

> Well, Claus, you fool, the great day's come at last!
> I'll kill you—(*Aside*) or they will. (*To* SANTA CLAUS.) Come, fight with me!

SANTA CLAUS:

> Aye, that I shall.

(*They start fighting. It is a mighty combat, a fight between elemental forces. At certain moments the combat ceases and one or the other speaks.*)

EASTER BUNNY:

> I have a feeling, fighting with this man,
> That I am fighting Death and Crime and Night.
> I sense an evil in his coming forth
> And in his moving back and to the sides.
> He terrifies me as none other does—
> But I shall fight him grandly, come what may!

SANTA CLAUS:

> This Easter Rabbit's Envy, Smut and Bile!
> Nothing has ever been, than him, more vile.
> It makes me weak with evil even to stand
> To fight with him, it weakens my good hand.

EASTER BUNNY:
He seems the natural force of all that's wrong.

SANTA CLAUS:
He is the dirty words to a good song!
Ah, Hatred guide my blows! and Justice, too!

FIRST COLD BACHELOR:
How goes the fight?

SECOND COLD BACHELOR:
It's even as of now.

FIRST COLD BACHELOR:
Our Lord will kill the old red bastard, sure!

SECOND COLD BACHELOR:
If not, our guns turn him to bird manure!

(*Enter the* SLIMY GREEN THINGS.)

EASTER BUNNY (*losing his strength*):
What—what's that? Help!

COLD BACHELORS:
Ah, help! help! help!

(*The* SLIMY GREEN THINGS *advance.* SANTA CLAUS *puts on his mask. The* EASTER BUNNY *and the* COLD BACHELORS *cough, grow faint, and sicken, then stumble or crawl away, followed by the* SLIMY GREEN THINGS. *Enter* LYN, *then* BOB.)

SANTA CLAUS:
Lyn, dear Lyn!

LYN:
Yes! Yes, I found them
In the northwestern section of this town
And me they followed hither.

BOB:
Bless your soul.

89

Where are the other Robins?

(*Enter* JILL, JIM, BUD, BILL, *and* LOUIS, *all of them worn out from their search for the* SLIMY GREEN THINGS.)

SANTA CLAUS:

Here they come,
And tired one and all, poor valiant stragglers!
(*All embrace.*)
Tonight we'll feast on octopus *galant*
Cooked by Wang Po, the best chef in Shanghai!
(*They go off.*)

ACT TWO

SCENE 1. *The terrace of the Coluhdson Hotel,*
a huge resort hotel in Asia. BOB, *alone.*

BOB (*reading aloud*):
>And one day her parents came to Asia, to the great hotel—
>It was a long time past. And a long time past, the father,
>The father who did not know what he knew,
>The father who took a fancy to the freshness and the sweetness of his girl,
>And the father who said to her, the mother willing it, too,
>"Dear, you must come home. . . ."

(JILL *and her* PARENTS *enter;* BOB *looks at them a moment, then leaves.*)

JILL'S FATHER:
>We want to meet him.

JILL:
>I don't know if that's possible. He's well—
>He is a little odder than you think—
>Or than you might think. He is rather fierce.

JILL'S MOTHER:
>Jill, dearest child, we want you to come home.

JILL'S FATHER:
> To this Coluhdson's walls from far away
> By airplane, camelback, canoe, and horse
> We've traveled, though we're middle-aged and weak-
> Er in some ways than you young people are
> Who call yourself Red Robins, just to say
> Jill, that we want you back, we want you home.

JILL:
> Dear parents, I do not think that I can.

COLUHDSON WAITER:
> Some goopah, Ma'am?

JILL'S MOTHER:
> What's that?

JILL:
> It is a native drink.

JILL'S FATHER:
>   Mm, well, no thank you.
> Well, yes, I'll have one, on the other hand.
> Jill, dear, you must come home.

JILL:
>   Don't think I can.

JILL'S FATHER:
> Would you like one of these cold goopahs, Mother?
> They're very cool and good.

JILL'S MOTHER:
>   Well, yes, I'll try one.

JILL'S FATHER:
> Make that two goopahs, waiter. And you, Jill?

JILL:
> I'll have a goopah, yes.

JILL'S FATHER:

                    Then that makes three.

JILL:

    I can't come home.

JILL'S FATHER:

    You must come home.
    Why should you have this senseless life out here
    When there is such a good life in the States
    Where you can live in peace and happiness,
    Secure and not surrounded by the jungle
    And apes and octopus and crazy birds,
    And puzzling people speaking alien tongues?
    Why should you have to live a life like this?
    We brought you up to be a regular girl.
    You can have anything you want, back home.
    What holds you here?

JILL'S MOTHER:

    People ask us. We're embarrassed.
    We don't know what to say.
    Why should Jill Brules be flying around Asia
    When other girls are getting engaged and married
    And having babies, making grandparents
    Of their proud, doting parents? We'd be happy
    If your young man would come back home with you.

JILL:

    Er—he is not so young. But to explain
    A little bit. One thing is I'm in love
    With Santa Claus—yes, yes, that is his name.
    Oh he's not the traditional one, of course,
    Not someone who goes flying off at Christmas
    As one is told he does when one's a child.
    He is a different one. At least, if he
    Is the traditional one, then everyone's
    Been misinformed as to what is his nature.
    He's a man
    So full of the excitement of his life
    That he seems more than human, like a god—

JILL'S MOTHER:

    That's sacrilegious.

    We have no right to speak of men like that.

    Please do not say such things.

JILL:

                   I'm sorry Mother

    I guess I'm just in love, like any girl,

    And guess I have exaggerated feelings

    As any other would. Well, that's not all, though.

    It isn't all that I'm so much in love.

    For I loved being a Red Robin when

    I first came out to be one, and when he

    Still roamed the savage North.

JILL'S FATHER:

    But it all seems so strange, and unconnected

    To you—and all you are!

JILL:

                   It isn't really.

    Do you remember—I do—all through childhood

    How much I loved to dance? And I remember

    A night in high school when the time was May,

    The term had almost ended, and, in white

    I danced with William Sansom and we whirled

    About the floor—we whirled, and whirled, and whirled—

    And I had the sensation that my movements

    Were like the movements of the waves and stars

    And were the only motions of the earth,

    Which, for our dancing, stopped. When in our airplanes,

    Or when in jungle converse with my friends,

    Or walking softly on the high plateaus

    Of Asia, I have these same feelings now—

    I feel, not a rejection of your life

    And all that is back home, but something stronger

    That makes me so much surer of *this* life.

JILL'S FATHER:

    Do all your young friends feel this way about it?

JILL:

> They all feel something.
> Something perhaps for all not quite the same,
> But strong enough to keep them here and happy—

JILL'S MOTHER:

> Well, it is nice they're here
> So you aren't all alone!

JILL'S FATHER:

> I say, let's meet this man, this Santa Claus!
> If he is worthy of you, we shall see.

JILL:

> I'll—try to get him.

JILL'S MOTHER:

> I'm sure that he will come.

JILL'S FATHER:

> Why shouldn't he? Are you ashamed of us?

JILL:

> No, Father, no. It's just that San—that he,
> Well, as I said, he is a little strange.
> He might be *violent*.

JILL'S FATHER:

> Then so might I!
> God damn, no man has rights over my daughter
> By violence and shall not be with me—
> No matter if he be Great Death Himself—
> Brutal or threatening in the slightest bit!
> I shall be violent with him, the clod,
> If he—

JILL'S MOTHER:

> Charles, stop. I'm sure that Jill's new friend
> If he loves her, will love or like us too.
> Go, get him, dearest. We will be waiting here.

JILL'S FATHER:

Yes, try to have him come here before lunch.
Then we can talk and then have lunch together.

JILL'S MOTHER:

Dear, it will be so nice.

JILL:

Well, well, I'll try.

(JILL *leaves her parents. As she is about to leave the Coluhdson terrace, she stops for a moment and speaks, as if she were musing, or reading aloud from a book.*)

A tender strain of violin music came floating to them on the steps of the Coluhdson as they sat there in the middle of the day, and Jill suddenly remembered it was spring. She remembered a May evening filled with frost-white butterflies and tulip-and-rose-bearing sticks.

(JILL *goes off.*)

JILL'S FATHER:

If I can talk some sense into his head,
And I do think I can, I think that we'll
Be going Stateside, dear, with a new son
And not have lost a daughter.

JILL'S MOTHER:

Well . . . I hope so.

JILL'S FATHER:

All shall be well.

SCENE 2. JILL'S MOTHER *and* FATHER, *at a table in the shade on the Coluhdson terrace, where they remain, silent, during this scene. Enter a* DOG.

DOG:

I am an animal, though civilized and domestic.
And I am not known. Yea, there is in my heart
That which is totally unknown to man.

96

Ah, Man, with his machines, his tools, his customs
Knows nothing of the generous, easy ways
We animals have nor knows he the nobility
That comes from being wholly without hope—
The secret of our being. And like a slave
Who follows a lord in haste and does not know
Where he is going, like a miser, too,
Who hurries after wealth which is his tyrant
And peace more quickly flees, so man pursues me,
Believes he tames me, takes me to his house
And chains me close, but does not know my heart,
And gives me food, but does not know my heart—
Wide open, generous, unsponsored, free—
And does not know, I think he does not know—
Believing that if, when called by him, I go,
He knows the best of me.

VOICE OFFSTAGE:

              Where's that damned beagle?
Oh, Christ! He's gotten loose in the hotel!
Here, Kahndor, come! Come Kahndor!

DOG:

              Rrrf! I will!

(DOG *runs off.*)

SCENE 3. *Still the Coluhdson terrace.*
SANTA CLAUS *enters, greets* JILL'S FATHER *and* MOTHER,
and joins them at a table. JILL *is not there.*

SANTA CLAUS:

I'm pleased to meet you, Sir, and hope that your
Trip has been good and that you're liking Asia.
There are so many grand things here to see.

JILL'S FATHER:

Why, yes, in fact we did have a good flight,
A good canoe trip and good camel ride.
We came here to see Jill, as you must know.

97

SANTA CLAUS:

    Of course she told me. Yes.

JILL'S FATHER:

                        This thing in Burma,
    This new political leader they have there,
    Sam Wando—what's his name

SANTA CLAUS:

                    Sanwandohfarris?

JILL'S FATHER:

    Yes, that's the fellow. Do you think he's good
    Or harmful? Did he win by an honest vote?

JILL'S MOTHER:

    Dear, that's all fine, but don't you think we should,
    Well, talk of Jill a little more?

SANTA CLAUS:

                    Miz Brules,
    I see now where your daughter got her smile
    And her blue eyes. They twinkle just like yours—
    And like the blue Pacific's waves, when they
    Are touched so gently by the summer dawn
    They show us pink and pearl as well as blue.
    Then daylight comes with his transforming hand
    And turns those tints to one engulfing hue,
    More various for so being.

JILL'S FATHER:

                    What? What's that?

SANTA CLAUS:

    And I believe—
    I see it in your eyes and so believe—
    It may be true, stout Sir, sweet Madame, that
    It is a life, too, would go well with you
    And you with it, could you but be persuaded
    To be Red Robins like ourselves. I think
    This broad expanse, these mountains' sides already

Have been persuasive, made you wish to stay.
You . . . have had such a thought?

JILL'S FATHER:

                        No, we'll go home
Not Robins, I should guess. You do seem confident
And Jill does too, and all the rest, you say,
This way of life is good.

SANTA CLAUS:

                        It is a way
Of life you may imagine and not live
And say such life is poetry, not life,
But once you've lived it for one day, one hour,
No other makes the slightest sense at all.

JILL'S MOTHER:

You, Sir, you really love her?

SANTA CLAUS:

Love, Madame, is my name.

JILL'S FATHER:

                    This Wandohfarris
You think he's a good man?

SANTA CLAUS:

                    He is all right.
We met last summer at the Hunters Club
Outside of Horror Burma's batwing region
And spoke of economics. He's first rate
In that. Don't know if he knows people, though,
As well as he knows finance.

JILL'S FATHER:

                  Hmm, that will
Be interesting to see, if he works out.
Mother, call Jill. She said she'd be downstairs
Near the front desk. It's time to have our lunch
And speak of something lighter.

(JILL'S MOTHER *leaves*. JILL'S FATHER *soliloquizes*.)

                 By my judgment
This is a good man. He'll be good to her.

(JILL *comes in, with her* MOTHER.)

    Jill, darling!

SANTA CLAUS:
    May I order?

JILL (*aside, to* SANTA CLAUS):
    Is everything all right?

SANTA CLAUS:
    I think it is.

JILL'S MOTHER (*answering* SANTA CLAUS):
       Yes, please.

SANTA CLAUS:
               I know the restaurant
And know the chef. I would suggest the Burmese Badger
As a main course, with pickled octopus
As a first course. Then pilot's salad after,
Mousse Tour Eiffel for sweet, then Burmese Coffee.

JILL'S FATHER:
    Sounds good.

(SANTA CLAUS *looks up and sees something alarming in the sky. He jumps to his feet, agitated.*)

SANTA CLAUS:
       Alas, I cannot stay with you,
For I have urgent business in the sky.

JILL'S MOTHER:
    What? What?

JILL'S FATHER:
What's this?

SANTA CLAUS:
There is a sign
Of light in that far stratosphere that shows
The Blood-Filled Rakes are screaming through the air
Of Lower Asia, heading for this place
And I must up before them and bring down
Their prideful feathers, leading to their doom.
Sweet parents of my Jill, a warm farewell
And my excuses. I have liked so much
To meet you, and I hope you will be here
When I get back. If not, good voyage home.

JILL:
Dear, must you? Yes, I see that you must go.

SANTA CLAUS:
Dear friends, farewell. (*He goes, swiftly.*)

JILL'S MOTHER:
He is a most unusual man.

JILL'S FATHER:
He seems a sensible one, and if you love him—

JILL:
I'm worried about him so, but yes, I do.

SCENE 4. *A beach, in Asia, and the Pacific Ocean,*
with a steamboat. The RED ROBINS *are gathered*
on the beach, ready for departure.

BOB:
Our next stop's Occhu Bocchu and its mountains,
Amidst which we'll find Aplaganda Lake,
With Congers Island in the midst of it
Where at this time—it's Maytime—of the year
The octopus hold solemn festival

And shriek and crawl about the savage rocks.

LYN:

How wonderful to see it! Jim and I
Will go there on the boat. We have our tickets.

BOB:

We'll see you there. The rest of us will fly.
Good luck. Good voyage. I know you love the ocean,
But do be careful as you're going there.
For octopus *en marche* from everywhere
Are gathering for fiesta.

JIM:

We'll take care.

(ROBINS *go off to their planes;* JIM *and* LYN *go aboard the boat;* JIM *goes below;* LYN *stands looking over the side.*)

LYN:

Happy I'll be to make this trip but happier
To make another one. Of my bad dreams
One is the chief, that I shall die before,
Or shall grow old, weary, or weak before
I see that fabled city of the East
Known as Tin Fan, which old philosophers hold
Is the external form of what is best
In this our universe. Its golden streets,
Or else not gold but asphalt, concrete, dirt,
Whatever they may be, they must be streets
Which lead to the fulfillment of desires
Before one even knows one has them, and
Its buildings, filled with feelings and ideas,
Its music and its statues and its forms
Of public celebration, and the life
Of its least citizen fill me with fire
To think of, and my chest and forehead burn
With the extreme desire to feel myself
Be there, and turn amidst its sights and sounds.

(*Music plays, and a* VOICE *speaks.*)

VOICE:

In the interior of China, I exist.
I am Cathay, Tin Fan, or what you wish
To call me by. I will not come. For you
Must come to me by sky and ocean blue
And over land,on rivers, come by mountains,
A million snowy mountains to the North,
Ten million snowy mountains to the South,
And a long winding river in between
With islands on it, on which can be seen
Small huts of grass and little chairs and tables
At which sit those who will not come so far
As you must come because some special feeling
Makes it the great necessity for you.
I am Tin Fan. I am Cathay. Extreme
The pleasures I propose. Extreme the dangers
You must go through to find me—chiefly, one:
That you will not believe that I exist.
At last, you'll not believe that I exist
And you'll give up the search. If you do not,
I'll make you happy for eternity.

(OCTOPUS *appear.*)

OCTOPUS:

We are the Octopus, and we are not known!
We're here to make you drown before you go!

LYN (*Not noticing the* OCTOPUS—*dreamily*):
That voice! I heard that voice! It was Tin Fan!

(*Now she notices the* OCTOPUS, *who are threatening.*)

Help! Octopus! They'll squeeze me till I'm dead
And leave me at the mercy of the Sea!

(*Enter* JIM, *concernedly.*)

JIM:

Octopus!
Down! Stay your pods! Oh, Lyn! Are you all right?

Down, slimy, damn you, octopus! Disgust!

(*The* OCTOPUS *withdraw.*)

OCTOPUS:

We weren't really doing any harm—
Just wanted a little kiss!

JIM:

That you shan't have!
Down, damn you, down! To Congers Island go,
Where sliminess is all the way of life!

OCTOPUS:

Ungrateful! You were saved by slimy things
That time in Shanghai of the Golden Stairs.

JIM:

That time is past. Besides, they were not you.

OCTOPUS:

How do you know they weren't? The prejudice
All human creatures have against the slime
That is the source of life, the space and time
Of embryos and all that vaunted lot,
Is vicious, unfair, and destructive as
A glass of Malay poison drunk at dawn.
We are but what you have forgotten once
You were, but grow away from every year:
Love's precious cold miasmic source of life.

JIM:

Perhaps. But you've no reason to hug Lyn!
God damn you, down! She is my girl, not yours!

OCTOPUS:

Well, we'll away. Remember us, though. Give our cares a thought.

(OCTOPUS *leave.*)

JIM:

Their cares a thought! Good God!

LYN:

Jim, I think I
Heard something from Tin Fan. Jim, we must go there!
Oh we must try to get there if we can!

JIM:

Lyn! Dearest! You're all right? Of course we'll go there!
We will do all we can!

(*He kisses her. Enter* CAPTAIN, *holding a letter.*)
Well—who are you? The captain—

CAPTAIN:

Of this boat.
I hate to interrupt you, but this note,
This precious note I have within my hand
Is from the ruler of a mighty land
And is addressed to someone he calls "Lyn."
Do you know such a person? Is it she,
As somehow I suspect that it may be?
If not, I beg your pardon. In any case,
I'm sorry to interrupt your private parley—

LYN:

My name is Lyn. You say a ruler. Is—

(*A musical flourish.*)

CAPTAIN:

It is the President of the United States,
Whose dream you are. He bade me bring you this.

(*He hands her the letter.* LYN *starts to read it and is frightened.* JIM *takes the letter from her, starts to read, and he too is frightened. Suddenly, an* APE *leaps up to them and seizes the letter.*)

APE:

Ha! ha! Now mine!

(APE *jumps overboard and swims off.*)

LYN:

    Got

JIM:

        to get

CAPTAIN:

            it back!

LYN:

                Oh God! God! God!

(*Blackout. Spotlight now shows* APE *on shore with the letter.* APE *pulls off his mask. It is the* EASTER BUNNY.)

EASTER BUNNY:

    Ha ha! This letter so incriminates
    Lyn and the President of the United States
    That in it I can taste my full revenge
    Against democracy and Robins both—
    And this will be the DEATH of Santa Claus!

S C E N E 5.   *An Airfield near Lake Aplaganda.*
Sky above. BOB *stands apart from the other* RED ROBINS.

BOB (*thinking aloud*):

    It is over.
    The Octopanorama's at an end
    Which we came here to witness. In the sky
    Are many things I love. But here on land
    It's Jill, and only she. Somehow together
    In this odd place, I think we may have found
    A reason, if there is one, to stay upon the ground!
    And yet not quite
    Has she been wholly mine. And now, too late!

(*An Airgram is delivered to* BOB. *He calls to the other* RED ROBINS.)

Jill! Everyone! We're summoned
By airgram, by an Englishman named Terrence
Who promises to show us Unfound Island!

OTHER RED ROBINS:

Good! Away!

BOB:

I think the route that's best is that one over
Isola Pushner. Now—into the planes!

(*All run off. Then, very shortly thereafter,* BOB *reappears, in his plane, in the sky.*)

BOB:

In the sky, and this is something that has been noticed before, everything
seems to be all right. Coming back to land, though, can often be a trial.
Balzac wanted everything—fame, money, love, power, acceptance—and
he was able to get them all. Yet he was tormented. Byron was born an
aristocrat; he was wealthy, handsome—and a great genius. Yet Byron led
a miserable life. Tennyson, too, was an unhappy man, in love with his
landlady's son.

The most remarkable thing about the sky is that there seems to be
nothing there, and this probably has something to do with the feeling of
happiness (or perhaps it is only euphoria) which is produced in a person
by being there. When Jill and I have our planes close together up high,
that is a moment I love. Conversation is often impossible to hear but
sometimes seems to have a celestial quality when one is flying.

I wonder if Napoleon was happy—and Homer. Nobody even knows
where Homer was born. There are three "Homeric birthplaces" in
Greece. Nobody is even sure that Homer wrote the *Odyssey*. Apparently,
he was blind. Like us, he was a sailor, though not a sailor of the sky.

Jesus Christ, perhaps the most influential man who ever lived, was
almost certainly extremely unhappy. Socrates was unhappy. I guess you
think Mao Tse-tung was a happy man. He was suffering from gastric
ulcers and could scarcely ascend the ancient speaking mound. The fact
that we are betrothed to old age and death is enough to make all people
unhappy.

In the air, I feel occupied. There is the steering, there are the controls,
there is that sense of being "above it all" yet participating in it in the most
lively and exhilarating way. I wonder if "escape" is the right word, as
someone once suggested when I talked of these things, for something

which so wholly absorbs the being and which requires so much skill, and
which brings so much of life into one small span. The countries that float
by down beneath me are like chapters in a book; and I feel them, and
what is in the air above them, in my face, and in my heart, and in my
mind.

SCENE 6.   *A small Pacific island.* MEINHEER PUSHNER, *an old Colonial*
official, is there, with his two NATIVE BEARERS.

FIRST NATIVE BEARER:
Meinheer Pushner, let me take you a little further in out of the cold. It's a
cool morning this is after being for the jungle, and you no longer a young
man, though a great man you have been after being and having been and
a great one still are, to my lights and by those of all other living beings
that knows of your name.

SECOND BEARER:
Of your existence and your name.

MEINHEER PUSHNER:
Yes, Manawa, and yes, Bonoro, thank you for what you say.
And thank you too for the concern you are after for being having just now
for me.

(*The* RED ROBINS' *planes fly over. He looks up at them.*)

But as the chilly waters of the blue Pacific swell
And scratch with morning light, I want to see
The birds as they fly overhead.

FIRST BEARER:
Oh my God, Sir, those are not real birds!

MEINHEER PUSHNER:
Manawa, who are we to say? and how are we to know?
Have I, in all these years here on the island, taught you nothing
But respect for me? I wanted to teach you also independent thought.
These may or may not be birds.
The important thing is that we do not know.

SECOND BEARER:

Those are Red Robins, Master.

MEINHEER PUSHNER (*musing*):

And there is one among them
Named Jill, whom I will always love!

FIRST BEARER:

Ah, yes, Master. She of whom you have spoken so often, in the island
evenings!

> S C E N E 7. *L'Isola Non Trovata, a beautiful Pacific island
> filled with flowers.* JILL *is there alone with a bunch of flowers
> she has picked.* TERRENCE, *an Englishman, and the other*
> RED ROBINS *enter on the other side of the island, not seeing* JILL.
> *Also present is the* EASTER BUNNY, *whom no one sees—
> perhaps very far to one side, away from the action.*

TERRENCE:

These giant flowers on your left are what
Is most amazing on this Unfound Island—
Isola Non Trovata to Gozzano,
The Italian poet who first used its name—
These flowers are said to be the origin
Of colors and of the human alphabet—
Somehow the vowels have been derived from them
And consonants from their leaves.

LYN:

What beautiful flowers!

BOB:

              They seem somehow to mean
More than a flower could mean. . . .

JILL (*coming over to the other* ROBINS: *looking at the flowers in her hand*):
A, black; E, white; I, red; U, green; O, blue. O vowels!
I see you now and now know where you come from—
Vowels are colors, which I'll now explain.

BOB:

What? Jill!
You've picked some flowers? Jill—

BUNNY (*unheard by others*):

I planned all this,
And this will bring them to a tragic doom.

LYN:

Is she all right?

BOB:

She seems to be in some sort of a trance!

TERRENCE:

It seems to be some magic of the island
That doth affect her thus—the Vowel Flowers.

(*Now* JILL *gives people flowers, one at a time, starting with* BOB. *To* BOB *she gives a black flower, to* LYN *a white one, to* JIM *a red one, to* LOUIS *a green one. She keeps the blue flower for herself. Each person who has a flower looks at it and speaks.*)

BOB:

A, Black. Chess pieces, licorice, funeral clothes;
Full note, half note, banana bruise, ape nose.

LYN:

E, White. Albumen, chiffon, blanks, cashmere;
White swimsuit-covered breasts; Tin Fan grown clear.

JIM:

I, Red. Nails, bitten lips, sunrise-tipped airways;
Deep re-created red of Shanghai stairways.

LOUIS:

U, Green. Eyelids, green ink, a praying mantis;
Costume of Pan, the opposite of Santa's.

JILL:

O, Blue. Smoke, goggles, air-reflecting things;
Eyes, linen and silk shirts, engagement rings.

(JILL *runs off.*)

BILL:
>Jill! Come back!
>She's going too far inland.

(*Distant ape sounds are heard.*)

BOB:
What? That shout—!

(*Now huge grunts and groans are heard.*)

>Jesus Christ! I think it is the Apes of Banzona!

BUD:
>Have we come to the wrong island?

TERRENCE:
I—I don't know—

BILL:
>You —!

(*He unmasks* TERRENCE, *who, beneath mask, turns out to be an ape.*)

BOB:
Quick! Got to rescue Jill—

(BOB *runs off and runs back on, tugging* JILL, *who is very frightened. Now* APES *advance onto the stage. Their leader,* FIRST APE, *walks up to* BOB.)

FIRST APE:
>No one shall resist the Apes of Banzona!
>Whoever sets foot on this island must die!

BOB:
>We shall see, insane rodents
>Of human size, we shall see!

LOUIS:

    Yet, enemies, stop!
    Why should we groups do battle with each other
    And cause much harm to bodies, leave some dead
    And others maimed and bleeding? Can we not,
    Instead, make some agreements? I propose
    We give each other tokens of esteem
    And drink some heady beverage of the island,
    Then we depart in peace.

BOB:

                  They want to kill us!

JIM:

    Stay, Robins stay. The words that Louis says
    Are true enough if the apes but accept them.

FIRST APE:

    You have invaded
    Our sacred island precincts. You must die.

SECOND APE:

    But, Lord, these are fair words the stranger speaks.
    Shall we not bend old custom to sweet peace
    And friendly gestures?

BILL:

                Part of which, for us,
    Will be returning to you this same traitor
    Who brought us here.

(*He pushes* "TERRENCE" *forward.*)

FIRST APE (*recognizing him*):
              Medoga Banzonino!
    You! seeking power still! brought them to fight
    On this most gracious Admiralty Island
    Unknown to all but us!

TERRENCE:

                I did and hoped

> They'd kill you, after which I would take power
> And use my fellow apes to conquer earth
> And drive all other beings into Hell!

FIRST APE:

> Take him to dungeon. And there let him be
> Treated with cacao and betel juice
> Till he return to reason. Then with trial
> Severe but fair we shall adjudge his case.
> Meanwhile, fair-haired strangers,
> Pardon, and welcome to these ape-brushed shores.
> Let ape musicians come, young ape and apess
> To wreathe these strangers' heads with vowel flowers
> A, E, I, O, and U. But Jill, who picked
> These flowers, must spend five months upon this island
> Each year, one month per flower.

BOB:

> She will not!

FIRST APE:

> Why damn you, then!

BOB:

> And you, god damn!

(BOB *and* FIRST APE *start to fight.*)

SECOND APE:

> Lord, stay your hand! Dear strangers, we wish nothing!
> Combating so, you play into the hand
> Of foul Medoga, who stands seething here
> Awash with grins like an old pot that's boiling
> Until its water's swirling. We cannot
> Blame one for picking flowers here which have
> On everyone a strange unknown effect,
> Making them irresistible to hands.

FIRST APE:

> All right. I humbly do apologize again.

BOB:

> Which we accept. Now make we merry, friends,
> For we must be in China by nightfall.

(*The* APES *and the* RED ROBINS *drink and dance.*)

EASTER BUNNY (*unseen and unheard by others*):

> So fails my plan! Dull peace has won the day.
> I must destroy them in another way!

(*He goes off.*)

ACT THREE

SCENE 1.   *A high place, with a small pavilion, in China.*
The RED ROBINS *are together.* JILL *is reading from a book.*

JILL (*reading*):
> And a man in a yellow coat, a tall man holding in his hand an excellent
> green tobacco cigar, was standing in the boat-house doorway. Was saying,
> "I do not think the gulls will fly this year." Or was saying, "I do think
> they will fly, will fly very high, so high above our sights, our heads, and
> heavens, that we shall never see them." And the blue dregs from his cigar
> like the ashes of the sea. "Shall fly high, and we shall never see them, so
> that to us it shall be as if they had never flown at all." That's beautiful!

(*Enter* LOUIS, *excited.*)

LOUIS:
> Quickly! into the Seat House! Ni Shu has come,
> The Chinese philosopher has come,
> And with him Santa Claus and the President!

(*Enter* NI SHU *with his retinue. Then enter* SANTA CLAUS *and the* PRESIDENT. *The*
PRESIDENT *is holding the Ring of Destiny.* LYN *sees it.*)

LYN (*to herself*):
> The Ring of Destiny!

PRESIDENT:

How hot it is, Santa Claus! Is it always this hot out here?

SANTA CLAUS:

It varies, your Lordship. Sometimes the jungle is very cool.
Once we almost froze to death.

PRESIDENT:

I should be very very sorry to hear of that!

(*Enter* MIKE THE TIGER.)

MIKE THE TIGER:

My name is Mike the Tiger.

(SANTA CLAUS *shoots* MIKE, *and he is dragged off.*)

PRESIDENT:

What was that?

SANTA CLAUS:

A man-eating tiger who's been bothering us.

PRESIDENT:

Good Lord!

LYN (*coming up to them*):

Mr. President—

PRESIDENT:

My God, it's—Lyn!

LYN:

Mr. President, hand me that ring!

PRESIDENT:

No! Never! It contains the secret of life. I haven't had time to use it yet or
even much time to look at or study it, really, but it's mine. I'm just too
busy, so far, to devote my time to it. But I'm going to. I don't want to give
it to anyone. After all, I'm the god-damned fucking President of the All

States Whites and I have a perfect right to every fucking thing in the universe that I wish!

JILL:

Which President are you?

PRESIDENT:

Oh my God! Fuck! I forgot! I'm no longer President!

(*He runs away into the jungle.*)

LYN:

Follow him! We've got to get that ring!

(*She starts to run after him, but* SANTA CLAUS *stops her.*)

SANTA CLAUS:

No! Let him go. The sado-masochistic jungle will do him in, and we'll have that ring tomorrow or the next day.

LYN:

You don't understand how important it is.

SANTA CLAUS:

I think I may.
And I think you may not understand how unimportant it is.
Now all must go to sleep.

BILL:

Wait, Mr. Santa Claus. You forgot about Ni Shu's being here.
Isn't he going to talk with us? Isn't that what this visit is all about?

NI SHU:

Yes, that is so.

SANTA CLAUS:

Sir, aren't you too disturbed by what has happened?

NI SHU:

No, I am never so. I am not rattled
By such events. For this same life and death

We feel about us now and in us now
Will always be here, whether we are here
Breathing its salt and lilac, or are not,
Seeing its red and yellow or are not,
Hearing its breathy splashing. And once we know
Our separation from and oneness with it,
We can endure whatever it may bring
And go on talking, go on functioning.

JILL:

How brave a thing it is to hear a man
Speak like an angel and render thin as air
The problems that destroy us every day!

SANTA CLAUS:

Well, then, my Lord, sit down and speak to us.

BILL:

Let us dispose ourselves upon the banks
Of this high wide pavilion and take on
The wisdom of the universe.

NI SHU:

Well, thanks.

(NI SHU *is seated in the pavilion, the* RED ROBINS *and* SANTA CLAUS *on the rocks and grass around it.*)

NI SHU:

Let us proceed this way, that you ask me
Short questions and in brief I shall reply.
That way we'll deal with more and keep things lively.
You have a question, you?

JILL:

What is life?

NI SHU:

It is a combination of the future
With old regrets, chained to a grinding engine
Of body's truck, which clambers up a hill.

BILL:

What then is love in life?

NI SHU:

Love is an essence
Which people think about in various cultures
In different ways, according to their views.
But always there is an element in love
Of selflessness or seeming selflessness,
Aggrandizement from giving of oneself—
Sometimes, it seems that one could say, a means—
To put it otherwise—of being free
Of what's most monstrous in the selfish self
By caring more for someone else. This can be
Attended by such shaking of the body that
One knows not what one is.

BOB:

Do you believe
Love, as you have described it, puts a person,
From being outside himself, in a more true
Relation with the world? Since all about us
There are so many things—skies, jungles, apes—
Which are not we ourselves?

NI SHU:

Yes, you could say so,
And said so I believe it were well said.

BILL:

Does our adventuring, then, here in the jungle
And in the skies and out upon the sea
To distant islands filled with strangest creatures,
Do our adventures bring us close to love
Or, failing that, close to the true estate
Of persons in the universe? Or would
A Stateside life be better—working hard
And raising children, acting out our part
In some already staked-out cultural plan?
That is, are we being fools to be Red Robins
And live the way we do?

NI SHU:

                        No one can answer.
Final evaluation of the self
Or what seems to be but is not the self
Must rest with something past the powers of man.
And how you'd grow a soul to be your best one
I do not know. But I suspect you know,
As I do, for myself. This lofty jungle
With its o'ertopping sky, this sensual freedom,
In which like raspberries steeped in their juice
You may so love each other, seems to be,
Surely, the life you love. And, loving it,
You're parted from your selfish selves and brought
Back to the self you'd be, if you could choose.

LYN:

What of Tin Fan? Shouldn't we try to go there?
Some people say so.

NI SHU:

                    I can't speak of it.
I'm sorry but it seems I have to go.
I have a consultation in Shanghai
At seven-thirty. Santa, can you fly me?
Dear young people, farewell!

LYN:

                    But I was asking—

BOB:

Shh. Lynn, he's obviously set against it.
He doesn't want to talk about it.

LYN:

                        But—

SANTA CLAUS:

Course I can, Master.
It's been a joy for us to have you here.

NI SHU:

> And for me too. Your young people are trenchant,
> Intelligent, and wise. They please me much.

BOB:

> Thank you, Master. Thank you from us all.

SANTA CLAUS:

> I'll fly Ni Shu to Shanghai. Meanwhile, dear ones,
> You all should get some sleep. Tomorrow will
> Be difficult and bloody, or else I
> Am a poor prophet.

BILL:

> Aye, aye, Sir, we shall.

(SANTA CLAUS *and* NI SHU *leave. It grows dark. The* RED ROBINS *lie down around the pavilion and go to sleep.*)

SCENE 2. *A high, rocky desert place in Asia. The* EASTER BUNNY *summons and then addresses his followers, in this instance the* SHARDS.

EASTER BUNNY:

> Thanks, my good helpers, for assembling here.
> As you know, very soon the time will come
> When we must meet in battle with the Robins
> And totally destroy them every one.
> And we must do it quickly, for they are
> Every day drawing nearer to Tin Fan,
> Which they must never reach, or else the earth
> Will be a mass of rubble. It is believed
> That if they get there, life will be destroyed.
> Our victory will not be an easy thing—
> For they have elements extremely strong
> Among them. There's no air fighter like Bob
> In any other outfit on the earth
> Nor is there any girl as smart as Jill
> Nor any, save myself, like Santa Claus
> For pure ferocity of flesh and spirit.
> He is a monster of increasing size,

A dreadful visitation on this earth
Where human eyes, deceived, conceive him kind
And generous, think he brings gifts to children
At cold December's finish, while the truth
Is that he is the cruelest to mankind
Of any person ever—

(PRESIDENT *runs in with the Ring.*)

What, you here?
You, whom the letter clearly showed to be
The ally of those Robins whom I hate?
Take this, and live no more!

(*He shoots him. The* PRESIDENT *falls down dead.*)

Let him be buried
With greatest pomp. He was our President—
Or theirs—somebody's—or in any case
So he has been reputed. Wait—I think
I may have murdered the wrong man. I think
This may not be the President at all!

(EASTER BUNNY *is troubled.*)

Well, give this man some honors, that his spirit
May go wherever it deserves to be
In heaven or hell, and then come back to listen
To all I'll tell you here.

FIRST, SECOND *and* THIRD SHARDS:
Aye, Mastering Lord!

(*They go off.*)

EASTER BUNNY:
Go off, you rest, as well. This thing upsets me.
I need some quiet with myself alone.

OTHER SHARDS:
Great Leader, yes.

(*All other* SHARDS *leave.*)

EASTER BUNNY:

What have I come to be

If murder, which is held the foulest crime
Of any in the universe, has come
To be my second nature, aye my first—
For I as soon would kill a man as not.
Is it my heritage from the animal world
Which I escaped by some Divine mistake
Or some Divine Intent unknown to me
Or anyone save Him who forms us all?
Oh I do not myself know what I am
And hate these moments of uncertainty
When I must speak of it. Better the life
Of violence and crime, far better a day
Filled with bright knives' sharp sides,the cannons' boom,
The leaden pellet splintering living bone,
The agony, the anguish, and the scream!
In such rough times I can forget my woes
And be the sacred rabbit of myself.
But, damn! Even I, because I'm part of life,
Although so freakish and so lost a part,
Must have self doubts and weep at what I am!
Well, we must win! My Shards! Great Shards, return!

(SHARDS *come back.*)

What battle we from henceforth shall indite
Let all be moved to wonder by! These stones
Which form this chain of mountains shall erupt
In fiery particles, which hence spewn forth
Shall burn this red-winged evil and consume!
All Asia shall turn poison to them. Touch
Whatever is, they die. And you, sad pieces
Of the Eternal Law, which now is broken,
Shatter their wings as you are shattered here!
Bring them to desperation! Twist their dreams
So that they have no hope!

SHARDS:

Aye, fatal Lord!

(*They go off.*)

SCENE 3. *A Clearing in the Jungle. Late night.*
BOB *has been sleeping; he gets up.*

BOB:

It's true, although I've said that it was not,
Told Jill and Bud and Bill that it was not,
That I am more unhappy than I think
It natural I should be. I do not know
Exactly why, though most from loving Jill
And being afraid I've lost her. Those first days,
Flying through Asia, how we loved each other!
Whole nights would turn to days and days to nights
And we would still be kissing. Occhu Bocchu
Filled suddenly with roses from our love
And Burma with regrets, for what we'd lost.
Yet still sometimes we have it, it is there,
I feel it, it is gone. Oh that I might
Meet toward the end of this deep jungle night
Some new endearing Presence, that could guide
Me to new love or Jill back to my side,
Or else make me forget it all and be
Absorbed in this profound intensity
Of Asian jungle dark undecked with stars!

(BIRD *appears.*)

BIRD:

I am a bird, a jungle bird. I am
Bird's true condition, always voyaging.

BOB:

A talking bird! You are a talking bird?

BIRD:

Each person has, some time, a talking bird.
At just one moment of each person's life,
Old books say (I believe them), man or woman,
The person has an intimate encounter
With what's non-human in the natural world.
This time of yours is now and is with me.

BOB:

>It is? It's true, I dreamed, when six years old
>And thereabouts, that I might learn the language
>Of birds and animals, and speak to them—
>Especially I wanted that of birds.

BIRD:

>What did you wish to say to us? or hear?

BOB:

>I wanted to know what it would be like
>To be non-human, to have colors, and
>To spread myself about, by wings, in space,
>But most of all to know some kind of freedom,
>Some special lightness, being rid of legs
>And chest and arms and back and knowing only
>The feeling of the air on every part.

BIRD:

>Have you experienced this at all as yet?

BOB:

>I have, in dreams, when, often, I can fly,
>Which I can start by running very fast.
>But only then—and then I am asleep.

(SANTA CLAUS *appears, on a terrace, looking out at a river.*)

SANTA CLAUS:

>Look how the Ho Ching River gently breaks
>Its silver lines in moonlight to the east!
>Oh for such beauty I would, sure, surrender
>My criminality, and love the world!
>But where is beauty when the moonlight's gone?
>Aye, there's the rub! In wealth and robbery!
>Ho Ching, good night!

BOB:

>Dear Bird, did you hear that?

BIRD:

> Hear what? Heard no
> One but yourself for I can only hear
> Your human words and not another's, no.
> But, what distracted you? What did you hear?

BOB:

> Heard Santa Claus, who's led us this far way,
> And who is loved by Jill—she whom I love—
> Speak of his criminality and evil,
> Which makes me fearful that some ill may come
> If we go on with him. Bird, you heard nothing?
> Something in how he said it made me fear—
> Could it have been a dream? My mind is troubled.
> Would you could tell me what this was and means!

BIRD:

> Gladly shall I inform you. Come with me
> Into this singing arbour, where we birds
> Are holding solemn colloquy tonight,
> A parliament of fowls, where we decide
> Each six-month all the most important questions
> Pertaining to our state. Come, follow me,
> And you may ask the question of us all!

(BOB *and* BIRD *go off. Loud singing of Birds.*)

SCENE 4. *A clearing.* JILL *is asleep.*
Enter a young MOTHER, *with a* CHILD *five or six years old.*
The MOTHER *and* CHILD *are dressed in a rather*
old-fashioned way. They are JILL'S *dream.*

MOTHER (*as if continuing a story*):

> But no one could ever really harm the Red Robins. You see, they had
> some kind of wonderful good luck, which always meant they'd come to
> no serious harm. Of course, that was not really the President that was
> killed, either. The real President was back in the capital, signing bills.
> The Red Robins! The Red Robins! Oh how we—I mean how they—
> loved islands! And the sky!

126

CHILD:

What were they like, Mommy?

MOTHER:

They were—Oh, I don't know, child, don't ask me. They were happier in a way than anyone else on the earth. (*She cries a little.*)

CHILD:

Oh Mommy! Don't cry. I'm sorry I asked you. Why is it so sad? Was it a long time ago?

MOTHER:

It seems a long time. But—it's all right. You can ask me anything you want. Come, what would you like to know?

CHILD:

I'm—I'm so sorry!

MOTHER:

You needn't be sorry, actually. I shouldn't be such a fool.
Why are you still beside me? Why aren't you off at school?

CHILD:

I'm not old enough yet, Mother.

MOTHER:

Oh, I'm sorry. Of course. Yes, we'd get into the planes, start the motors humming, and fly off regularly into the grey-pink evening sky!

CHILD:

Where would you land, Mother?

MOTHER:

Oh, in every sort of place! Islands, volcanic mountains, sometimes in fiery molten valleys hundreds of miles under the earth. Once there was a high place full of snowfalls, a terrace on which gulls served us lemonade, and high trumpets made a music out of stars.

CHILD:

Oh, if only I could see it!

MOTHER:

Do you want to go?

CHILD:

Go where, Mother? Go there, Mother? Oh Mother, I'd die to do it!

MOTHER:

You mustn't do that, child. Just stay. Grow older, a little older. Then we shall see. I will, if I can, then take you back myself—Chim Dek, Chim Dek—

CHILD:

What, Mother? Oh tell me, what did you say?

MOTHER:

I—I don't know. I am a foolish mother, a stupid girl. Listen, darling, I'm sorry. I don't know quite what I said.

CHILD:

I want to go!

MOTHER:

We cannot go, dearest. As far as being a Red Robin is concerned, either one is one or not. There is no way to get to be one.

(MOTHER *and* CHILD *go off, and* JILL *wakes up.* BOB *comes in and sits on a stone.* JILL *goes to him.*)

BOB (*to himself*):
I saw last night that Santa Claus was evil
And the birds told me there was no Tin Fan!

JILL (*her dream has made her very sad*):
Bob . . . let's go home.

BOB:

You, too? Yes, I've been feeling that we should.
Why do you want to?

JILL:

I don't know.

BOB:

> I think it's probably the best thing after all—
> Yes—I'll go tell the plan to everyone—
> We'll rendezvous in Shanghai and, from there,
> Take the long passage home. Jill, meet me here
> In half an hour, and we'll fly.

JILL:

> I will.

(BOB *leaves.* JILL *now speaks alone.*)

> Asia, good-bye! Travels, good-bye! And you,
> Hope of my life, my love, my Santa Claus,
> Forgive me, and good-bye! I don't quite know
> What takes me back, but do know I must go.

> SCENE 5. *The White House. Seated around a great table*
> *are the* PRESIDENT, JILL'S FATHER, *the* EASTER BUNNY
> (*disguised as* COUNT LAPIN, *a French nobleman*),
> *and* TERRENCE (*disguised as an* ENGLISH LORD).

PRESIDENT:

> It's a great pleasure, of course, to have convened
> A group of such distinguished persons here.
> Count Lapin, you are welcome, and you, Sir Terrence,
> Lord of Northumberland and Counties east
> And west of there. You, also, Henry Brules,
> Of Minneapolis, a businessman,
> The image and the model of what's best
> In the American way. Our subject is—

EASTER BUNNY:

> Sir, the Red Robins and the harm they've done
> And do your country by their voyagings!

PRESIDENT:

> Dear Count, what harm is that? It's always seemed
> To me they were benign, good, lovely birds,
> Both girls and boys, who seek the beau ideal,

The truth that lies beyond the sun and moon
Where luck and love are one.

TERRENCE:
                              Those are but dreams—
Proper to youth, perhaps—but only dreams!
The truth, dear Sir, is that when they're enacted
As they are by this foul, unlawful bunch,
They harm your nation's image—and the world.

PRESIDENT:
So bad as that? I do not think I know
What these proud boys and girls have done that is
Of harm to anyone.

EASTER BUNNY:
                              Sir, you must know it—
They've done much wrong! Have taunted apes; have planted
Rose seeds on Kinta Plain which grew so strongly
They forced all other vegetation out
And left the natives starving. This year, they
Brought snowstorms and all kinds of winter weather
Into the Burmese jungle, where before,
Even apes did sweat to climb. These are your "Robins"
You think so innocent!

TERRENCE:
And they have broken Attanwandu Island's
Enormous crystal eggs to look inside
For clues to where Tin Fan is, which, once known,
The earth will be destroyed!

PRESIDENT:
                              The earth destroyed . . . ?
That doesn't sound to me like them at all!

JILL'S FATHER:
I don't believe it! My daughter never would—

PRESIDENT:
I do not think—

130

EASTER BUNNY:
Think! They have spoiled the image

Of that good, sweet United States you love!
I say this shame must stop!

TERRENCE:
And I agree!

JILL'S FATHER:

Something of this that is too strong for me!
I am Jill's father, come to claim her back—
But you, God damn, I'll not hear her reviled
By such as you—and you—

(*He angrily attacks* TERRENCE *and the* EASTER BUNNY, *tearing at them, and thus reveals something of their true ape and bunny identities beneath their disguises.*)

EASTER BUNNY:
Why damn you, I—

PRESIDENT (*leaping to his feet*):
Stop! Instant! Peace!

(*He rings a bell. Enter* WHITE HOUSE POLICEMEN, *who sieze* TERRENCE *and* EASTER BUNNY.)

Most furious officers, arrest these two!
(*Indicating the* EASTER BUNNY.)
Lock this one fast in prison. Heaviest chains
About him wind—for he is magical
And may have powers that go beyond those known
To human intellect. (*Indicating* TERRENCE.) This ape, once chained,
Load onto plane and fly to Unfound Island,
Where he'll be held by those who justly rule.
(*To* JILL'S FATHER.) Sir, I am sorry. I am much distracted.
What was your suit to me?

EASTER BUNNY (*aside*):
He knows too much!

How did he ever get to know so much?

(*To* PRESIDENT.) Believe me, President, you have not the power
To hold me here. The Robins all shall die!

PRESIDENT:
Take him away! Enough!

(*The* BUNNY *and* TERRENCE *are led off.*)

JILL'S FATHER:
I have a picture
Of Jill with the Red Robins. (*He hands a photograph to the* PRESIDENT.) I
have come
To ask you if my baby might come home.
I want her home. Mother is sad and lonely—
Her life seems nothing to her without Jill—

PRESIDENT:
Dear Sir, you once agreed to let her stay—
On the Coluhdson Terrace you agreed—

JILL'S FATHER:
How did you know?

PRESIDENT:
I know. But is it fair—?

JILL'S FATHER:
Feelings are fair, my Lord, howe'er they come!

PRESIDENT (*gazing at* LYN's *face in the photograph*):
True! True!
(*Aside.*) Oh, down, my surging heart! My pulse, lie still!
Lyn! Lyn! (*To* FATHER.) Perhaps I'll go there with you—and we'll see!

(*Great roaring, crashing, and flapping. Enter an* AIDE, *very upset.*)

AIDE:
The East—the Easter Bunny has escaped
And with him Terrence, clutched in his white arm!
He broke the White House walls and all the roofs
And, with one kicking punch, destroyed the work

That all First Ladies ever dreamed and did!

PRESIDENT:

(*Aside.*) Good God! Dear Lyn! To think she is in danger
Takes all my thoughts from me! (*To* AIDE.) Quick, Sirs, a plane!
I'll follow him!

AIDE:

          All planes are grounded, Sir,
By some strange palpitation of the air
Caused by the Easter Bunny!

JILL'S FATHER:

               Oh, Jill—

PRESIDENT:

                    Lyn!

AIDE:

     And scientists are saying—this is worse!—
That any flights attempted in or out
Of the United States for thirty days
Will end in engine failure, and in death!

PRESIDENT:

Alert the nation!

(*He goes off swiftly, followed by* JILL'S FATHER *and the* AIDE.)

        SCENE 6. *The streets of Shanghai.* JILL *has just arrived.*
             At the top of one of the Shanghai stairways are
              the MOTHER *and* CHILD *who were her dream.*

MOTHER (*to* CHILD):

Well, we got here just in time! We're with the Robins!

CHILD:

I like it! How beautiful everything is!

JILL:
> Shanghai!

MOTHER (*unseen and unheard by* JILL—*to the audience*):
> The Easter Bunny, when they were asleep,
> Gave all the worst of dreams. Jill's was of me—
> The Rabbit's evil powers summoned me
> From where I lived, to be in it, to be
> Herself, a mother, living in the States
> And not a Robin any more—remembering
> The life she'd had, wishing it would come back.
> And all the Robins were in fact the worse
> For what the Bunny'd done. They all decided
> Their life was useless and they should go home.

(*Enter* LYN, JIM, *and other* RED ROBINS, *separately.*)

LYN:
> *Should* we go home? Bob, I feel something . . . *wrong*—
> As if I were no longer sure, as if
> We were by going home somehow endangered.
> Do you suppose
> It all could be an Easter Bunny's trick?

BOB:
> How could we know? We have to do what we
> Are able to. I feel I can't go on.

(*The* EASTER BUNNY *appears. Only the* MOTHER *sees him.*)

EASTER BUNNY (*jubilantly*):
> Victory! Victory is mine!

(EASTER BUNNY *leaves.*)

MOTHER (*aside*):
> Not yours but mine,
> May be this victory, Bunny, after all!
> For I shall right whatever wrong I did
> And save my younger self, whose dream I was,
> And thus reverse the time.

(*To* JILL—*only* JILL *can see or hear her.*)
Jill, can you hear me? Jill, call Santa Claus!
It can be your salvation if you do.
Call Santa Claus.
Have you forgotten him? He has some powers
You've known, and loved, but he has others, too,
Some holiday power he has not used as yet,
With which I think that he can save you now.
Jill, call him! He's not far.

JILL:

Didn't I see you last night in my dream?

MOTHER:

You did. And you will never see me more
Unless you do arrive in Tin Fan, for
There I reside, in a white silvery building
Which looks out on the River of the Doors—
And *there* is Paradise. Beautiful Shanghai,
City of golden stairs—but as a cloud,
A shadow, or a memory, to Tin Fan!
Till you come there, farewell!

(MOTHER *and* CHILD *go off.*)

JILL:

Santa Claus, can you help us? Oh where are you?

BOB:

Jill, it is too late! We must go home!

(SANTA CLAUS *appears at the top of the stairs. While he speaks,* SANTA CLAUS
scatters snowflakes over the RED ROBINS, *reviving them both with the snowflakes
and with his magical words.*)

SANTA:

It's not too late. Because—
Get up everybody, we're going to go
To a place where there's sunshine and soft white snow—
To a place that's been perfect since time began—
We're going to take a journey to fabulous Tin Fan!

Tin Fan, Tin Fan, the old people say
Is the only place on earth that is also a Way!
So . . . ARISE!

(*The* RED ROBINS *are themselves again.*)

BOB:

What happened to us? What?

JIM:

Shanghai! The stairways!

JILL:

How strange! I can't believe that we gave up . . .

BOB (*to* SANTA CLAUS):

Santa Claus, I . . . apologize. I dreamed . . .
I dreamed last night . . . I thought . . . that you were evil.

SANTA CLAUS:

Sometimes I think it myself. You've done no harm.

BOB:

And there was something else as bad—or worse—
I was with birds and understood their language.
In some strange way they seemed to know the truth.
I asked them things. They answered me. They told me
That there was no Tin Fan!

LYN:

N-no Tin Fan!?

(*Sound of Birds.*)

The birds, though, may be lying after all
Out of wishing to keep Tin Fan for themselves!

BOB:

I never thought of that—that birds might lie.
But is that possible? Do birds and animals lie?

LYN:

I want to go and see!

JIM:

Of course we will.

(*Now a* VOICE *is heard, the* TIN FAN VOICE *that* LYN *heard in Act II, Scene 4, when she was on the boat.*)

VOICE:

I am Tin Fan. I am Cathay. Extreme
The pleasures I propose. Extreme the dangers
You must go through to find me—chiefly, one:
That you will not believe that I exist
And you'll give up the search. If you do not,
I'll make you happy for eternity.

(*A* MESSENGER *arrives and hands a letter to* JIM, *who opens it.*)

VARIOUS RED ROBINS:

Jim, what is it?

JIM (*dramatically*):

It's—it's a letter from Dr. Pep,
Inviting us all to come and visit him
At his plantation on the Azhakansee!
It is important. The President will be there
And other men and women filled with power
And fortune, who would fain investigate
The nature of our being on this earth.
So we should go.

BOB:

Then, quickly, into the planes!
Toward Dr. Pep—and all that mystery!

(*They fly off.*)

The banks of a Jungle River.
Enter MARIAN, *a native girl.*

MARIAN:

I am Marian, the native girl who is a sort of love slave to Dr. Pep. It was I who sent the message, which is mostly lies. But my God, I hope they come! My life here is unbearable. It will end. Only they can save me! Oh, I hope they will come!

(*She goes off.*)

SCENE 8. *They sky above Asia. It is late afternoon,*
changing to dark, and, with BOB's *entrance, dawn.*
The characters appear in the sky one by one—first, SANTA CLAUS.

SANTA CLAUS:

I am Night. I am Death.
I am the place where no one can follow.
They cannot know it.
My face and form do not show it.
I am Crime. I am Death.
I am Night. I am what never can be found.
Chim Dek.
I am master of all, of the day,
Of the year, of the hour.
Only at Christmas is my power seen,
And then it is misunderstood.
I am incapable of good
(Or of evil). I am Power.

(*Enter* JILL.)

JILL:

I am Life.
I cut the Christmas cake with a keen-bladed knife
And give it out unequally to the casual guests.
I am involved in everything that is best
And worst. I set standards for what I try
But my only negative judgment is to die.
Neither good nor evil am I,

In Boston or in Shanghai,
For I am Life.

(*Enter* LYN.)

LYN:

    I am Desire. I am Enchantment and Desire.
    Whenever, wherever I go there, there is fire.
    I burn and will consume. I startle the President in his living room,
    The hawk, and the acrobat on his high wire. I am Desire.

(*Enter* JIM.)

JIM:

    When will I find the peace of great experience?
    Where is the star I can follow
    That is not hollow, that brings me home again?
    I am Intellectual Desire, Aspiring Mind.
    I fly, criss-crossing earth and humankind.

(*Enter* EASTER BUNNY.)

EASTER BUNNY:

    I have infested these airplanes
    With a kind of dream gas
    So that no one will ever clearly know
    Exactly what things mean.
    By this, I expect to prevent
    Them from reaching their destinations!

(*Enter* BUD.)

BUD:

    Foolish as usual, our enemy miscalculates
    The nature of our mission—to mediate, to communicate
    To bridge the state between earth and the sky!
    Oh tell me, Apollo-Buddha,
    In what week are you fixing to linger
    In the white bony church of our feet?

(*Enter* LOUIS.)

LOUIS:

    In the peace of the night
    I am the thought of the day
    That is there, but cannot be seen.

(*Enter* BILL.)

BILL:

    I am the missing page of the magazine
    That prefigures light.
    I am the body, when it is strong as a stone.

(*Enter the* PRESIDENT, *walking slowly, holding a letter.*)

PRESIDENT:

    Forever, alone . . . Well, maybe not . . . I'll find her with this letter.

(PRESIDENT *walks off. Enter the* STARS.)

STARS:

    We are the Stars, and we are not known.
    Only at midnight is our power shown
    And then it is misunderstood.
    We do no evil, no good. We stay here to show
    As the Ocean stays below to show
    That what is not known
    Shows many ways to be, although it seems,
    Sometimes, that there is but one way alone.

(STARS *leave. It begins to grow light. Enter* BOB.)

BOB:

    Why do you seek me, god of the sickly wail
    And uneuphonious song? Is it that I and my kind
    Have offended you in the temples of hillocks?
    Of pillows? In the sky, everything is the controls
    And the whispering of sashes, like the way a bright eye flashes
    Or airplane crashes, which is the wind against the plane.

END

THE
STRANGERS
FROM
THE SEA

SCENE 1   *A comfortable apartment in Stockholm.*

Two persons SVEN *and* ANNA *are seated in chairs.*

SVEN:

> I think I'm going to kill myself.

ANNA:

> Don't! Play a game of "Ox" with me instead!
> Actually it's called "Strangers from the Sea."

SVEN:

> Oh, I know it! I played it as a child.

ANNA:

> Would you do me the favor of playing it once with me?

SVEN:

> What's the use?

ANNA:

> Will you?

SVEN:

> Let me think about it.

ANNA:

> Please.

SVEN:

> The very idea is fatiguing.

ANNA:

> I haven't asked you very many things.

SVEN:

> All right. But, I warn you, Anna, and this is the truth.
> This is the last thing I will ever do for you.

ANNA (*aside*):

> Pray God that it works well.
> (*to* SVEN)
> Yes, Sven, yes, thank you. All right.

SVEN:

> Then, let's begin.

SCENE 2. *The scene changes to the deck of a cattle boat off the coast of Sweden. Stormy sea. Mist. Spray. Stage right is Sweden, a dock. Enter the* OXEN OF HUNGARY.

OXEN:

> We want to be fed!

SHEPHERD:

> There is no way to feed you here.
> We are out in the middle of the ocean.

OXEN:

> Well, if we are not fed, we are not going to give any milk!

SHEPHERD:

> Oh hell—

CAPTAIN:

> Don't worry, Shepherd. I think we are getting near Sweden.
> In Sweden there is plenty of milk. And, besides,
> Since when do oxen give milk? And there will be
> Food for them there, anyway, food for the oxen.

144

ELLA (SHEPHERD's *girlfriend*):

> That's good. I want our oxen to have something to eat.

HAND:

> The boat is landing.

CAPTAIN:

> Good! Let's get these smelly oxen off!

AN OX:

> I heard what you said.

CAPTAIN:

> Well anyway you can't talk.
> And in the herd form you're in I don't see
> How you can do me much harm.

OX:

> Oh, nuts to you. Come on every-
> Body, let's get off.

LEAD OX:

> And hurry. Damn!

> (OXEN *and* HUMANS *all get off boat onto Swedish dock.*
> *The* OXEN *surround the* HUMANS.)

THIRD OX:
> Now

SECOND OX:
> We have

FIRST OX:
> You all!

CAPTAIN AND MATES:
> Wha-what's happened.

SHEPHERD:
> This is a little puzzling to me, too.

ELLA:

    But not so much to me.

LEAD OX:

    Damn! Salaam! Everybody out of the way—

(*Turmoil, as* OXEN *take over the country.*)

SWEDISH MAN:

    What— what's happened?

LEAD OX:

    The Oxen of Hungary have conquered Sweden.

        (*It grows dark—there are muffled sounds.*)

MINSTREL:

    And art will grow up
    And develop
             (*Dawn breaks.*)
    Under the oxen's yoke.
    I think they may be good for Sweden.

          (*Ten days pass.*)
    Sweden develops like an ox.
    That's good. It is good for Sweden
    To have these startling experiences.

SCENE 3.   *A group of singing* PEOPLE *and* OXEN *in a flower-filled field.*

ALL (*singing*):

    Happy the Swedish nation
    All her days
    Happy sensation
    Oxen children everywhere
    We will become the most beautiful
    People on earth
    Especially our women
    Beautiful from loving oxen
    What truly are oxen

146

ELLA (SHEPHERD*'s girlfriend*):

> That's good. I want our oxen to have something to eat.

HAND:

> The boat is landing.

CAPTAIN:

> Good! Let's get these smelly oxen off!

AN OX:

> I heard what you said.

CAPTAIN:

> Well anyway you can't talk.
> And in the herd form you're in I don't see
> How you can do me much harm.

OX:

> Oh, nuts to you. Come on every–
> Body, let's get off.

LEAD OX:

> And hurry. Damn!

> (OXEN *and* HUMANS *all get off boat onto Swedish dock.*
> *The* OXEN *surround the* HUMANS.)

THIRD OX:

> Now

SECOND OX:

> We have

FIRST OX:

> You all!

CAPTAIN AND MATES:

> Wha–what's happened.

SHEPHERD:

> This is a little puzzling to me, too.

ELLA:

But not so much to me.

LEAD OX:

Damn! Salaam! Everybody out of the way—

(*Turmoil, as* OXEN *take over the country.*)

SWEDISH MAN:

What— what's happened?

LEAD OX:

The Oxen of Hungary have conquered Sweden.

(*It grows dark—there are muffled sounds.*)

MINSTREL:

And art will grow up
And develop
(*Dawn breaks.*)
Under the oxen's yoke.
I think they may be good for Sweden.

(*Ten days pass.*)
Sweden develops like an ox.
That's good. It is good for Sweden
To have these startling experiences.

SCENE 3. *A group of singing* PEOPLE *and* OXEN *in a flower-filled field.*

ALL (*singing*):

Happy the Swedish nation
All her days
Happy sensation
Oxen children everywhere
We will become the most beautiful
People on earth
Especially our women
Beautiful from loving oxen
What truly are oxen

146

But men of great worth
Transformed to four-legg'd creatures
With bestial naive features
But these are changed by love!
Oh, this is a time of triumph
And a time for celebration
The oxen came to Sweden
They guide us to the future
To future love!
The oxen bring us power and bring us love!

(*All dance, then bow to one another.*)

SCENE 4. *Stockholm, main square.*
Enter SHEPHERD, ELLA, LEAD OX *and three other* LEAD OXEN.

SHEPHERD:

My oxen have occupied Sweden
They have mated with Swedish women
Soon many in Sweden will be half-ox.
They tell me now they must move on,
They are going to another country.
What will happen to Sweden in their absence?
The Swedish populace has learned to love these oxen.
They have named public buildings after them:
Ox Palace, over here to your right,
Formerly the Danschluss Ministry of Finance Complex
And here's Ox Museum,
Formerly the Royal Swedish Nursery.
Ordinary Swedish will be sad.

ELLA:

Yes, and the Royal Family is lamenting, too.
For the oxen brought order to Sweden
And gave it a mixture of the old and the new
And the animal and the man
Which has been helpful.
The King has named the royal roads of his realm
After oxen. Oxpath is the main road
That leads from Stockholm to the sea

And the highway that intercepts Upsala
Is now named Oxen of Death.

SHEPHERD:
> Oh this is history
> Truly being brought to life!
> These oxen have made little changes
> All over this country
> In ways that can scarcely be seen.

LEAD OX:
> I the Lead Ox
> Made love last night to Princess Nancy
> Of Sweden. She will bear me a half-ox son.

SECOND OX:
> And I, Second-in-Command Ox,
> Have decorated the country with ox chateaus—
> Simple, really. These
> Are little straw structures
> People can
> Come into, if they wish, to
> Shield their bodies
> From the rain.

THIRD OX:
> And the snow,
> Which is wild, in Sweden.
> And I, the Third Ox in command,
> Have had special
> Beds built all over the kingdom
> In which those who are
> Half ox can lie
> For soon they will need them!
> We oxes made love
> To so many girls!

FOURTH OX:
> It was easy for us to
> Learn the language!
> And for the people of Sweden to learn

148

And take sweet Ella for my bride.
You shall sail without my help
Over fields of salt and kelp
Till you find another land
To which you'll give a helping hand.
Ella and I will stay behind
And try to find
A little paradise of our own.

LEAD OX:

You speak like one with a head of stone.
You'd do better to accompany us but
Farewell! You've been a
Good enough shepherd.
Then, we needed one—
Now, obviously, we don't. Come
On, fellow oxen, let's get on the boat.

(*Once on the boat, the* OXEN *begin, violently, suddenly, to make the movements
and the sounds of real oxen.*)

OXEN:

Oonh oonh grow-pht row-pht—

ELLA:

They have turned back to ordinary oxen again!

SHEPHERD:

My god my god they are running amok on the boat

ELLA:

They have trampled the captain

SHEPHERD:

And all the sailors.

ELLA:

My

SHEPHERD:

God! Now

ELLA:

It's sailing away!

SHEPHERD:

And they are

ELLA:

Again just oxen

SHEPHERD:

Who don't know anything

ELLA:

And certainly not

SHEPHERD:

How to navigate a boat!

ELLA:

How can we help them?

SHEPHERD:

We can't!

ELLA:

The

SHEPHERD:

Boat is

ELLA:

Gone!

(*The* OXEN'*s boat becomes invisible. There is a large sound of lowing.*)

(*Enter* PRINCESS NANCY.)

PRINCESS NANCY:

Gone!
Wherever they have gone to
There shall I travel!

Wherever oxen go, shall Nancy follow.
Helmsman, set sail and follow! I'll board this ship!

(PRINCESS NANCY *boards ship and it sails away.*)

ELLA:

We can only remember how it was
Before the oxen came to Sweden. People were unhappy.
Now with the oxen and Nancy gone
They may be unhappy again.

SHEPHERD:

I prophesy
That what has so been done
In these proud days, shall never be undone.
The country is indelibly altered—
For the better, rather than for the worse—
And Princess Nancy shall return.

(SVEN *and* ANNA *enter.*)

SVEN (*solemnly*):

So ends The Strangers From the Sea.

SCENE 5. *A great wind blows, and suddenly the scene is
the Stockholm apartment of Scene 1.*

SVEN:

Whew! That was a good game.
Did it take longer than usual?

ANNA:

No it always takes the same amount of time.
It's just that we forget our country's history,
Its main events, how full of things they were!

SVEN:

Yes, truly.

ANNA:

Do you still feel so sad?

SVEN:

> Just a little,
> But the game has picked me up
> A little too! I feel a will to live.
> Thank you!

ANNA:

> Such great events
> Are strength not only in themselves but give
> Invigoration and the will to live
> To those who follow after
> And are indeed the strangers from the sea
> Themselves, unknown contingents that embark
> Descend and occupy and make the dark
> A light, and by their spell
> Show us that seeing well
> Such great things as have been
> Places us in the planetary spin
> That makes our lives worthwhile. Oh eeuuhhh oh euuhh
>> (ANNA *makes ox noises.*)
> Oh strangers from the sea!

END

THE
BANQUET

To Marcello Panni

*(The first scene is Paris streets, with two men—*JEAN-LUC *and* MICHEL*—walking along. The time is the present.)*

JEAN-LUC:

    I think I know the story just about
    By heart. I told it to Jean-Marc two days ago.
    He came up to me saying, Ah, Jean-Luc!
    I heard that you were present at the banquet
    Given toward the end of the War—Picasso was there,
    And Gertrude Stein, Marinetti, Satie, Cocteau,
    And Marie Laurencin and Apollinaire—
    Apollinaire's last banquet—and that everyone spoke of love.

MICHEL:

    Yes, that's the one I want to hear about.

JEAN-LUC:

    Well, it was very silly of Jean-Marc
    To think I could have been at that banquet. I said, Look at me
    Do you think I'm old enough to have been there?
    It was in nineteen eighteen. No, I heard the story
    From André Salmon, who *was* there. He said there were a whole
    Lot of other people there, too—Max Jacob, Philippe Soupault,
    Alice B. Toklas, Pablo's Fernande—but only seven of them spoke—
    And how they spoke—and sang—of love!

MICHEL:

    Tell me everything about it. That night seems certainly like the last night
    Of something, and like the first night of something else. Tell me what the
        speeches were, and the songs.

JEAN-LUC:

> Well, according to André Salmon, they were something like this—but I
>> think it might be better
> To show you what I saw, as if it were actually there in front of me,
> When Salmon told me the story. He said he had gone with Picasso to the
>> Closerie des Lilas
> Which had been all set up for the occasion. He said "Everyone was excited.
> I hadn't been planning to go, but Pablo talked me into it. He said
>> Apollinaire would probably come.
> However, when we got there, Guillaume was the only one not present—
>> there were Jean Cocteau,
> Eric Satie, who was in charge of it, Filippo Tomasso Marinetti, up
> From Italy for the event, and Marie Laurencin, quite amazingly having
>> traveled there from Spain,
> Leaving her husband and everything, just to come and talk about love—
> Or perhaps no, really, they didn't even know before they got there
> That they were going to talk about love—I guess she came just for the
>> company
> And maybe to see Guillaume, though that part didn't turn out well.
> In any case, she was there and looking beautiful, and Gertrude Stein was
> There too, with Alice B. Toklas and some sheets of paper
> As if *she* would be ready to speak about anything, and of course Picasso,
> But no Guillaume. We knew, of course, about his injury
> But Satie seemed confident anyway that he would come. It was Satie who
>> proposed, after we got there,
> The subject of what they'd say. We were, aside from Apollinaire, the last
>> ones to get there."

*(The scene changes to the Closerie, the beginning of the Banquet. Drinking,
merriment, and singing. The* CHORUS, *or* EVERYONE *more or less, is singing The
Banquet Song. Over the din of this song,* SATIE *welcomes the new arrivals,* PICASSO,
FERNANDE, *and* SALMON.*)*

THE BANQUET SONG

> Ah, sweet Banquet, lovely Banquet
> From your seats you get your name
> From the bench, banchetto, banquette
> But from love you get your fame
> Love and drink and song and friendship
> We extol you from our benches

Banquet, Banquet, holy Banquet
Here the spirit is transcendent
Joined by wine and wit and laughter
No one soul is independent
All are joined in one enormous
Vision of the life before us

Ah sweet banquet thank you thank you
Banquet hear our glasses ring
We shall do our best to make you
A fiesta'd everything
Such a banquet as has never
Been and which will last forever!

SATIE:

Welcome, Pablo and Fernande. Ah, André! How good that you could come!
Our party's just begun. Tonight
Each one of us is going to give a toast
And speak in praise of love.

PICASSO:

Splendid idea!

COCTEAU:

Pablo, welcome. Ah, Fernande. Et toi, mon cher Salmon!

PICASSO:

Cocteau, it's good to see you.
What a party!

SATIE:

From Italy we've drawn
This mighty Marinetti!

MARINETTI (*imitating a racing-car engine on his rolled* r*'s; he is wearing a racing-car helmet*):
Buona Sera, ovvero buooona serrrra to you all!

PICASSO:

Gertrude, you are on my wall, or rather you are on your wall—
I painted you, and you are on your wall—how nice to see you here!

STEIN:

> Alice and I decided to walk out, is it? Is to visit
> And get a little tremble from Paree.

PICASSO:

> Dear Marie Laurencin!

MARIE LAURENCIN:

> Pablo! Pablo!

SATIE:

> Come, come, now let's sit down. And we'll begin.

(*All the* GUESTS *now sit down at a big lavishly spread table with bottles of wine and all sorts of plates, glasses, etc. Waiters move in and out and there is much festive serving and consuming of food and drink. There is silence, though, while the characters speak and sing. After each speaker's song, the festive noise breaks out again.* SATIE, *who is a sort of master of the revels, is seated in the center; it is he who calls on the others to speak. In front of* SATIE, *on or under the table, or perhaps to one side, is a very small piano keyboard, on which he may play notes to punctuate the end of a speech or song, to call on a new speaker, to illustrate and accompany his own speech and song, or for any other reason.*)

SATIE:

> I've told you my idea,
> That each of us should speak in praise of love.
> Perhaps the world can use new ways of looking
> At love since Plato set the subject cooking
> In Greece twenty five hundred years ago—

PICASSO:

> Ah, we do need Guillaume!
> He is our living expert on the subject.

MARIE LAURENCIN (*aside*):

> Well, I don't know . . .

VARIOUS GUESTS:

> Guillaume, what, not arrived yet? Non. Non. Oui.

(*Now there is a sudden silence as everyone realizes that* APOLLINAIRE *is not there.*)

VARIOUS GUESTS:

>Where, where is Gui?
>Where is Guillaume Apollinaire
>Our reigning poet and great banqueteer?

(*Another silence.*)

COCTEAU:

>He isn't here
>I asked him but he isn't here

SATIE:

>And I asked him—he isn't here

MARINETTI:

>Is he too ill? Is his wound bad again?

MARIE LAURENCIN:

>I heard that he was better—ill again?

PICASSO:

>Past time and past loves do not come again
>But something tells me Guillaume will appear—

MARIE LAURENCIN:

>I did hear he was better—

PICASSO:

>Before the evening's done—with us again.

SATIE:

>I think you're right. He can speak later. He always likes, in any case, to play the most dramatic part in any street, cafe, or theatre. A late dramatic entrance suits him fine. If he does come . . . But let's begin! Silence! A toast: to Love!

(ALL *lift their glasses, some saying or singing "Love"; others "Amore" or "Amour"*)

SATIE:

>Picasso, I've decided. You are first.

PICASSO:

Thank you, Eric Satie. In love, as in painting, what is important is not to
search but to find. I hate the search, I hate the concept of searching.
What decent artist, what decent lover, ever spent his time in the search?
Search is for ninnies. The point, if you are a serious man, is to find. I find
a woman as I find a subject—here she is! Now to change her, to vary her,
to cover the walls of my heart with her, that's it! And one day's work leads
to another. It's tomorrow and it's time to begin again. It's constant action.
I keep finding out who she is, who I am, what It is—such is Love. Love is
finding and it is changes, and its changes are its seductions. It at last, it
always adds up, it is a sum—but a sum of destructions. This is how I love
and how I paint.

ARIA

Love is a sum
Of destructions
A woman standing naked in the sun
Is not in need of introductions
You see her she sees you
What do you do? When I have no red, I use blue.

In love there is no one
Consummation
Assorted demoiselles of Avignon
Are made of color and sensation
You see them they see you
What do you do? When I have no red, I use blue.

Though in love there is perfection,
It is not what's in your mind
When you take your first direction—
But in what at last you find!

PICASSO (*speaking again*):

And that is the beginning and the end of what I have to say. For this
instant. Let's drink!

SATIE (*to* STEIN *who, it can now be seen, has a big pile of papers in front of her on
the table*):

Fair lady of Fleurus, will you speak next
After this dark and barbarous man of Spain?

STEIN:

Will I will yes and thank you. I will use these papers I won't. Thank you. I won't use these papers because love is simple and yet to talk about love is simple and yet to talk about love is not is it not it is not simple. These papers are recipes. Sometimes recipes are simple. A cat and a dog in a pie is not simple. Love is simple.

(*She hands the papers to* ALICE B. TOKLAS *who puts them away in a big purse.*)

Love is as it is. In this way it is simple. But is it simple is it is it is it. Writing is simple it is less simple. Is it simple to write. To write is less simple. In writing one must begin again and again. Again and again and again and again and again. Again begin. Begin with a blue shovel. Again is simple it is not so simple. And include everything is this simple is this love. I say writing but it is also love. It is that simple. Is love simple is it simple. It is simple because it is not and we get used to it. I say love is simple because it is not and we get used to it. We get used to its being what it is not. I may say. And that is love is writing beginning and beginning without writing. Is it. It is simple to sing of love. And praise praise it.

ARIA

What is love is it is it is it
Is it it is is it is it simple
There is is there blue sky above
Above roof above above roof
Not where I expect to be
The first time me you see

Love is Ladies Voices
Act Three
Love is Four Saints
Ask me
Love is Lifting Belly
Thank you points to it

Thank you for love naturally
Which every single day I see
Act One The birds fly
Act Four You and I
Act Two Stay with me
Act Three is Act Five

SATIE:

Thank you, Lady of Sentences. Your prose is your prose is your prose. As for your poetry, I'm all envy for my songs. Quelles delicieuses pièces froides!

STEIN:

I thank you thank you.

SATIE (*to* COCTEAU):

Jean. Can you speak next? By the way, Happy Birthday!

ALL:

Bonne anniversaire! bonne fête! and happy birthday!

(*A cake, decorated with angels and motorcyclists and with 29 candles, is brought in and set before* COCTEAU.)

SATIE:

Do you, at the old age you reach today,
At twenty-nine, do you think, have something left to say?

COCTEAU:

Thanks for the cake. Merci pour ce gateau. As for my old age, Eric, it's not so funny. Well, you have almost twice my age. I guess it may be funny for you. But it's a sadness of life that we grow old. Love is something else. Love is always young, it's always new, and that, my dear teacher and funny man, and all the rest of you great talents around, is because it remains unknown—it is a mystery. That keeps it young. It is a mystery and it is a secret. Even when you find out the secret of love, you are left with the mystery. And of a mystery we can never have too much. It is always there, entreating us, to solve it, to be lost in it, to rejoice in it. From this, its eternal youth. Not paralleled, alas, by our own. We grow old, and love stays there the same, like an eternal sailor, or, rather, like a young one. And now he is transformed to an angel, that is the mystery, and he has wings made of wood, that is the secret, and he has an arm like the capital neck of a swan, and that is the beauty, and he is disheveled, and that is the chance occurence, and he is in his shirtsleeves, and that is to be expected, and he looks like a sailboat when it is sinking, and that is the end, which is to say, it is the beginning of love. Its blue eyes go straight through my heart.

164

ARIA

Love, love, composed
Of angels, of cyclists, of swans,
Of great marble statues with no clothes on,
And of the Virgin Mary and the soda-water siphon—
You fizz and you bubble in New York
And in Paris and where ships come into port.

In Dakar and in Marseilles
How you shine in each café!
You're a blue Negro who boxes
Equators as well as equinoxes.
You're the Little American Girl and the Sailor—
Beaux clowns vous êtes fox terriers!

And now you are an angel in shirtsleeves with the neck of a swan
On the Champs Elysées, at a café you're sitting down—
Is it too late, or will you give me the time of day?
For I'm twenty-nine, and time is almost gone!

SATIE:

Well, so! A toast to Jean! May he have many poetic returns of the day!

(*to* MARINETTI)

Marinetti, here you've been with your helmet on all this time. What news do you bring us from the future? Is it dangerous? Should we all be protecting our heads?

MARINETTI:

Basta l'umore. Et basta spaghetti et basta l'amore del passato. It is the FUTURE that determines the nature of love. Enough of the love of the past—all that useless paraphernalia! It is time to break through to the truth—of love and of everything else. In our factory-filled streets, with their sounds of machines, odor of smoke, in the distance noises of cannon,

(*Noise of* CANNON—*from the War—may be heard here.*)

with cars chasing by and airplanes overhead, look! who are these two, dressed in laces and frills, speaking to each other so plaintively, in

165

measured verse, about *rondini* and *i piccini fiorini* and who knows what other *inininini*—and he plays—a mandolin! *Iddio mio,* and she, she lets fall her perfumed hankie into the street. The dump truck will pick it up! It is going to hit them, those two sappy lovers! They've crept here from another epoch, and they'll have to go back. Such lovers cannot be us. No! Love of the Future, you are a Love of steel. The man is a welder, and the woman is fire. You are violent and burning, and clear. No old sadness, no old treacheries, no secret meetings, no lovenotes—edged with tears! and with perfume! that silly poison—Pfui! Pfooah! It is *your* perfume, New Love, that impels us, propels us, drives us upwards and outwards into the air. You, perfume of the exhaust of a car, like the exhalations of angels, angels with wings like iron trenchers. I sing to the future, I sing my song of love to a car, to my *iddio di una razza d'acciaio,* to my racing car!

ARIA

Veemente Dio d'una razza d'acciaio
Automobile ebbrrra di spazio
che scalpiti e Frrremy d'angoscia
rodendo il morso con striduli denti
It is You that I love and who are Love!

Dieu véhément d'une race d'acier
Automobile ivre d'espace
qui piétines d'angoisse,
rongeant le mors aux dents stridentes
It is You that I love and who are Love!

Vehement God of a steel race
Automobile drunk on space
you pawing the road and braking with anguish
champing at the bit with strident teeth
It's You that I love
                    and who are Love!

MARINETTI:

That's my song.

(*To* SATIE)

Satie, you speak next. I want to hear what *you* have to say, you who have been somewhat bossing us around.

SATIE:

Well, it seems more polite to me to let Marie—

MARINETTI:

I don't see why—

PICASSO (*to* SATIE):

Eric, why don't you speak? And let Marie be later. We may yet see Gui. Better if what she says is when he's here.

SATIE:

All right. So be it. I have mainly just one idea. It's about lightness. What if love is, truly, light? Of course love is supposed to be heavy and deep, and in its heaviness and in its depths to bring sorrow and pain. Well, what if that is all a mistake, and the truth about love is that like certain music, like the music I am writing for my *Socrate,* love is essentially light and white—blank, *blanc.* Listen, and you'll hear what I think love can be, what I think love is. Love came in a shimmering white dress and gave this idea to me. Or so it seemed. But in truth she was dressed very simply and said it to me as if it were a joke.

ARIA

I have a girl in the form of a pear
She has thirty-two simple measures
In two/four time
And she is mine
Each morning when I sing to her, she's mine—
"Biqui," je dis, "ma poire!"—such simple pleasures!

When I sit down to write her an air
It is always full of syncopations
If love is blind,
It isn't mine
Each movement of it's in piano time—
Tink tank tunk tank tank tunk—such elations!

Run, run, my fingers, up and sideways,
Pedal here and silence there—
Love, and music, always find ways
To be shaped and make a pear—
Love, like music, makes a pair!

SATIE:

Marie?

MARIE LAURENCIN:

Beautiful, Eric. But Love hasn't been light for me. It's been adventurous,
but rather heavy and strong. "Entre les fauves et les cubistes / Prise au
piège, petite biche." Between the Fauvists and the Cubists, that was me,
caught in a trap, like a little deer. That's how Cocteau described me in a
poem and I suppose it describes my artistic position pretty well.
Guillaume was more flattering. He made me out to be some sort of
delirious delectably eternally feminine painter, the female possessor of
qualities not before present in the art of man. Well, that's how I seemed
to be to them. Picasso ran into me in 1907 and he said to Apollinaire, "I
think I've found you a fiancée!" Guillaume took him up on it, took *me* up
on *him*. I hope my mother doesn't hear that! She's very proper. She didn't
at all approve of Gui and my other Bohemian friends. Gui says I broke
his heart. He was all the time a little bit breaking mine. He's sometimes a
rather cruel and eccentric man. I envisioned something else—

(*At this moment the door opens and* APOLLINAIRE *enters. He has a white bandage
around his head.* MARIE LAURENCIN *stops speaking, as does everyone else. Then
there is great excitement. Everyone at the banquet has been waiting for him to
come.*)

SATIE:

Guillaume!

PICASSO:

Guillaume!

OTHERS:

Guillaume! Guillaume! Apollinaire!

APOLLINAIRE:

    Hello! How much I've wanted to be here
    In this last Banquet Year!

COCTEAU:

    Your injury—from the War—?

APOLLINAIRE:

    That hurts me much less than it did before.

SATIE:

    How goes the war for France?

APOLLINAIRE:

    Our troops and theirs advance
    Our planes meet in explosions like great roses
    Whose petals fall on Nancy and Coblentz!
    I'm sorry to be late.

SATIE:

    Sit down, sit down!
    We have been waiting for you but you're not too late. Everyone is giving a
    little talk about love. You'll be next, if you wish—after Marie.

(APOLLINAIRE *turns and sees* MARIE LAURENCIN.)

APOLLINAIRE (*very agitatedly*):
    Marie! Marie ma Laurencin!

SATIE:

    Marie had just begun—

APOLLINAIRE:

    Marie! You, here!

MARIE LAURENCIN:

    Bonsoir, Guillaume!

APOLLINAIRE:

    My Frizzy-head! my Standing-over-there!

My heart is broken like my head, Marie—
Oh my one only love, come back to me!

MARIE LAURENCIN:

I can't, Guillaume.

SATIE:

Gui, let her finish what she has to say, what she began to say—Then it's
your turn to speak. You can say—anything.

MARIE LAURENCIN:

It's, it's hard to talk of love when Gui is here. Well, well, I'll try. . . . The
truth is, when I think of Love, Love seems to have Gui's face, that
extraordinary face shaped like a pear. And Love has his lightness and his
jokes. In other ways, Love is not Gui at all. Gui is in love with change,
and what he loved in me was change. That's good for poetry—but not,
for me, for love.

ARIA

Under the Mirabeau Bridge flowed the Seine
I went away and I came back again
You loved me this way and you loved me that way
Nothing wholly made us happy
Like that river I can't go back again
Under the Mirabeau Bridge flowed the Seine.

You wrote, "Oh when will you come back Marie—
Quand donc reviendrez-vous Marie"
And wrote, "Ah when will this week ever end—
Quand donc finira la semaine"
You wrote when I was gone most beautifully
What had it, though, Guillaume, to do with me?

White days flow from us and light words from you
And from my brushes lines of red and blue.
I paint you with Picasso and Fernande—
I'm in it, too, a flower in my hand.
That moment's there, it cannot come again.
Under the Mirabeau Bridge flows the Seine.

APOLLINAIRE:

Marie, that's terrible! What you say about our love is terrible! Marie, it isn't true.

MARIE LAURENCIN:

Gui, I learned all of that from you—
Everything I said I got from you:
That nothing lasts and no one can be true—
It's all from you.

APOLLINAIRE:

Not fair, Marie, not true. I wrote that poem after I had lost you.
Having you was the truth of love for me.
I want that truth again!

MARIE LAURENCIN:

But I can't come back, Gui.

APOLLINAIRE:

Still, I have my chance to speak. Oh, Marie, let me persuade you! Let my speech and my poetry persuade you. That is, I suppose, what poetry is all about. But has it ever been more serious, more put to the test than this? And it's so hard for me to speak about love, quite aside from the fact that I have already done so so much. It's hard for me to speak because love is almost everything I am. I don't exist apart from it. I am all kinds of it. I am made up of a thousand kinds of love. Do you know that there is no word for *horse* in the Arabic language? But that there are one hundred, at least, for different kinds of horses? That is how it is with love and me. I am love nostalgic, love sadistic, love longing, and love delicacy, I am love violent, love unbounded, I am love playful, I am love absconded, love with and without rhyme, I am love obscure, love clarity, I am love peculiarity. Do you remember making love in my bedroom, Marie? We couldn't use the bed, I'd only let us use the chair. We were happy there.

MARIE LAURENCIN (*speaking aside*):

Yes, I was happy there
But can't be any longer.

APOLLINAIRE:

Oh, love
You've given me my best poetry and you

Have been best comfort when with women or alone.
You were my sweet companion all through *Zone*—
When I walked through Paris, Love, with you
And my warm fresh sense of Marie there too

MARIE LAURENCIN (*to* APOLLINAIRE):
   You were in love with losing me, and change.

APOLLINAIRE (*to* MARIE LAURENCIN):
   Marie . . . I feel change. That's not quite to say I love it. I look at the river
   flowing, and I feel love. But it's not for the river. A man can't simply
   attach himself to change. He needs a woman, a woman who embodies
   that change. To feel that flowing in one dear person one can hold in one's
   arms. Without that, I'm not a poet, I'm not anything!

ARIA

   Not war not aircraft guns not injury
   Not time not change not age but just your leaving me
   Deprives me of my self Marie
   O Mona Lisa of Modernity
   My love my luck my twentieth century
   Marie Marie Marie come back to me

MARIE LAURENCIN:
   I can't, Guillaume.

   Not that great shepherdess the Tour Eiffel
   Not Notre Dame with its enormous bell
   That praises heaven down as deep as hell
   Not Botticelli's lady on the shell
   Nor any other can give back to me
   What you could if you wished me well Marie

MARIE LAURENCIN:
   I do, but can't, Guillaume.

   Marie I've seen the century turn and change
   I've seen this century's art become as strange
   As any ever was in history
   There never was so beautiful and strange

172

A moment at this present century
So found by me now lost in you Marie

MARIE LAURENCIN:
  In you and me!

(*Now* APOLLINAIRE *sings his Aria again, and this time* MARIE LAURENCIN *joins in with hers—"Under the Mirabeau Bridge flowed the Seine," etc. So they are singing a Duet of these two Arias. Next,* APOLLINAIRE *sings the following Aria. It may be sung as a Duet with* MARIE LAURENCIN's *Aria; or, perhaps,* APOLLINAIRE *sings it alone first and then sings again the last stanza—"Let the days pass . . . Seine"— while* MARIE LAURENCIN *sings the first stanza of her Aria.*)

APOLLINAIRE ARIA #2

  Let us be hand in hand
  And face to face
  While underneath the bridge
  That our arms make passes
  The worn-out weary flow
  Of unending glances.

  L'amour s'en va
  Like that rushing water
  Love goes away
  Comme cette eau courante
  How slow life is comme la vie est lente
  How violent is hope comme l'esperance est violente

  Let the days pass let the weeks pass
  Neither time past
  Nor loves come back again
  Under the Mirabeau Bridge flows the Seine

APOLLINAIRE (*crying out, at the end of the Duet*):
  Unless————!

(*Now there is loud knocking at the door of the Café, and the sounds of an enormous festive Paris* CROWD *outside.*)

KNOCK KNOCK

STEIN:

What's all the noise outside?

COCTEAU:

It's Paris—but Paris all excited. About what?

KNOCK KNOCK KNOCK KNOCK

(SATIE *goes to the door and opens it*)

SATIE:

What is this all about?

THE CROWD OUTSIDE:

There's good news of the War! It soon may be over! Let us in!

SATIE:

Come in, come in!

(*People throng into the Closerie. Recognizable among the new celebrants are* JOSEPHINE BAKER, ANDRE BRETON, PAUL ELUARD, TRISTAN TZARA, DARIUS MILHAUD, ERNEST HEMINGWAY, SCOTT *and* ZELDA FITZGERALD, MAX ERNST, FRANCIS PICABIA, *and other notable participants in artistic life in Paris in the 1920's and 1930's. They are a sort of Chorus representing the Times to Come, like the Chorus of Athenian Women at the end of Aeschylus's* Oresteia.)

MEMBERS OF THE NEW CROWD:

Let's drink!
                    We'll drink!
Come on!
                    We'll drink!

SATIE:

Come in! Our revels now are ended.

ANDRE BRETON:

No! Beginning.

PICABIA:

Our revels now begin!

174

STEIN:

Welcome well welcome.

MEMBERS OF THE CROWD:

Well, we'll drink!

SATIE:

Come in!

PICABIA:

Let's sing of love!

(*Now the* CROWD, *led by* JOSEPHINE BAKER, *sings.*)

SONG

Love is a flower
It lasts for an hour
Ah the sweet moment
So quickly over

VARIOUS VOICES:

Love is a heart attack
Love is an almanac
Love is a breaking back
Well, love is, obviously, anything you like

SATIE:

I'd say not quite.
Our talk tonight has been but a beginning.

PICASSO:

Who knows as this young century goes spinning
Through interstellar night
If anything more new, or true, of love will come to light?

APOLLINAIRE (*to* MARIE LAURENCIN):

One chance, Marie!

SATIE (*answering* PICASSO):

That we must wait and see!

(Now all becomes quiet, and there is a Last Song, sung by PICASSO, STEIN, COCTEAU, MARINETTI, SATIE, MARIE LAURENCIN, *and* APOLLINAIRE.)

LAST SONG

When I have no red, I use blue

What is love is it is it is it
Is it is it it is is it simple
Is it too late?
I'm twenty-nine, and time is almost gone

Automobile drunk on space
Pawing the road and braking with anguish
It's you that I love

She has thirty-two simple measures
In two/four time—such simple pleasures!

Love is a sum of destructions

You wrote, "Oh when will you come back Marie"
And from my brushes lines of red and blue

And now you are an angel in shirtsleeves with the neck of a swan

Neither time past nor love comes back again
Under the Mirabeau Bridge flows the Seine

(Curtain.)

A HEROINE
OF THE
GREEK
RESISTANCE

K (A MAN):

    My first trip to Greece and I don't have any buttons
    On my one good shirt so I wear a "tee-shirt" with over it a suit jacket
    And this dumb English guy I'm with, there are about four of us,
    Says, "It's not correct!"
    Well, it would be all the fad later
    But he was probably right then that it wasn't "correct."
    I came back, to Nice, gratis, on a Greek army plane, with a heroine of the
        Greek Resistance.
    She is a good person is simple, even rudimentary.
    I go with her to a restaurant in Nice where the waiter wants her to order a
        whole dinner.
    "Il le faut, mademoiselle," but she won't do it. She doesn't want to and
        she doesn't have much money.
    Neither do I or I would treat her. Even If I'd been broke I should have
        treated her
    But I was worried about the train fare to Paris. Instead, I told the waiter
    That she was a heroine of the Greek Resistance. This had no effect at all.
    I think what she and I did was to share one dinner. I think I paid for it
        after all.
    The waiter was a little furious. But you can't sit here Msieu (or
        Mademoiselle!)
    I thought, He can't tell which one of us is eating. I was arrogant about my
        French.
    I said again She is a heroine of the Greek Résistance
    As if he and I would automatically be in complicity about this
    Recognize my niceness his cordiality her heroism
    And that (meal) would be that. I forget if it wasn't or was
    But one of these scenarios did take place
    As so often happens. I was wearing the jacket and tee-shirt then as well.

SPIRIT OF TIME:

      Each with its moments, the old tower in the center of the city was eaten
          away
      By restoration, the moon cake of fiery bracelets, but
      On the rooftop cafe there was a scene
      I will not long remember: a lightning bug
      Carried up accidentally on the rim of a drinking glass
      Flew off and vanished into bug invisibility of air.
      To move that trembling from a firm today
      Into a griped tomorrow like a sleeve
      Caught in Grand Central doorway,
      And mock-up of today. This edifice,
      This tangy corps of green, this swipe, this England
      Affording men a murder day, once seen
      Once tackled into nothingness, bristly and giving orderly
      Commands to leggy multitudes, O here
      Is someone to command your briefest breath, Mahatma Shakespeare
      The birds in the carolling of rest. But there is someone else around here
      I stallingly want you to meet, my brother in fact, hemlock.
      Over the hay cart into the flaring scenes
      Is as close as hemlock gets. "My dear, holloa!" In Martinique
      The birds that woke up in net stockings warbling loud and clear
      Focussed the steeple's eyes on the murrain—

K:

      Hume's ghost! I don't want Hume's ghost! Off, out of here!
      Away goes, flies Hume's ghost. These sparkling strains
      Of unencumbered music like the flood
      I cannot speak. Move something. I cannot move. Do
      Something. I cannot do
      Nothing. The master is ill-educated. Away! Get him a job in the English
          Department of stars!
      Let the working-men and -women fully their fray
      Indict to waving branches, I am yours
      On flossy emphasis
      Zoroaster blasts away:
      You just not doing the fucking job here, he said, and when Bleeps!
      Why it even catches me as much as the Flood. To west, adventure,
          fountains dead
      And eagle of the first good-bye, who stood there waiting
      The tray and the bed also were waiting. Then comes an engine,

Behind it a whole train. In it an engineer, his wife, a baby
Everyone assumes is his and hers, she keeps a pageboy
Bob worn by Ginger Rogers in nineteen thirty six. My claim is talkies,
Western the sides of the sea. This is childhood thought. But of a very
    specific childhood.
A violence without brothers and sisters, no superintendent—
The next day after this I got on the train
That took me to Paris.
It turned out to be some sort of continuation of the Orient Express
Is that possible
When I dressed so boldly it wasn't imitation it was desperation
V. the Chinese eating everything out of necessity the French out of
    curiosity
Disparition of the buttons

SPIRIT OF TIME:

    Where is he now
    Who once was vinylmaster of the fields? Dead bark
    Water on books. Evenings that go too far.
    Deep, and narrow, nine feet tall
    At the extremities, and seventy five yards long. A green prospect
    Stretches it may be ever outward, but their songs
    Of all different families, singing, the bluebirds there. Life is fortune
    But talk straight. She promises him an envelope.
    He is leading the stairs. A scimitar crops the Pope's hair. Good Christ!
    Mannikins start to be hobbled on the Champs Elysées.

K:

    My father said, I like the start of it but what are you going to do to make
      it end?
    The Greek woman staring at the shake of the early morning on the tie-
      clip sea
    We shouldn't wear—will she marry? Innocence! and despair!

FATHER:

    No one can really accomplish anything
    Who doesn't get up early in the morning.

K:

    But I said I need the late night and early morning
    The grip, father, and to get a grip on all the laws

And flaws of this kind of well don't you agree mortifying existence
Girls turning me down, jobs hard to get, insolence on the barges,
Late-night sheet pounding, the whole god-damned lot don't
Swear, the mother said. Organized villages
Clamped into stores, one city contained in a shop,
Country and even continent contained in a boat, life is yours!
I was finished with the adding machines of Lake Constance.
Yes, I was a latter-day walking.
I wanted the city to enfold me like a vote
For myself and itself: co-owners of the derby.
Flying among the grapes, bees sense a miracle
It is ordinary life. So, men and women, boys, and girls, sealions and their
    masters
And the dog's bark. What's "bourgeois" or extraordinary about any of
    these?
Everyone gets to walk
A little ways. Burning, burning, the collegiate amanuensis
A numbing hunger which she sees, then
Where is Napoleon?—intimacy, but she was shepherds
In her own field, the classy anatomy—who said sheaf?
A blond bird on a redheaded stone is sleeping. Give me your poor
Your damaged your inveterate.

DANTE:

Useful, the moon beneath our feet.

MODERNITY:

I spoke for Dagwood Bumstead,
For Jungle Jim, for Maggie and Jiggs, for all those roasted customers
In comic strips who never could unbend—these sharpening tricksters
These hucksters of the values of the soul
This eye that crosses everywhere is England
Like baby chickens colored useless for Easter
Then hatched into an egg again, slowly developing dyes
A gray, great factor, one of three
Justly celebrated acrobats, the gay yellow one there with his sister
Adumbelavara the corn king's mirthful equivalence
But what comes home and what comes back to me
Is something as out-of-the-ordinary as the Annunciation—
A grave asphyxiated by Lake Erie.

YOUNG WOMAN:
    "Jove in the clouds—"

MODERNITY:
    A young woman is trying to quote a song,
    Of nineteen fifty six when the door mattered
    And the teeth mattered and the flowers chattered of Americanism
    Bonuses, Williams and the dead, we were jovial and timeless
    But lived to cultivate those hours
    At five o'clock in the morning, when no one was there
    Have you looked for the Amazon forests? they're sleeping, like busts in a
        hall
    Like animals in the catalogue of stars.
    Greek numen, come home!
    With rapturous expressions, beaming "Home!"

K:
    My father then looked at the Charles and said "I like it
    And its Cambridge along with it. Superior people
    Never make long visits. Piebald lived in a glass house.
    Turra lurra lurra is an old people's dovecote, nonetheless."
    "Home is here, freedom from Boss Prendergast
    And every other thing. But here is home!" to stagger into existence
    Janus in the janissary, Comus in the man—
    Necklaces that prance into the dimness
    Because of the rumor "Hellas is transparent" and they let you do this
    Occasionally the whole day long, the worst not being in it
    Because it is afraid of the best or else if suffering puts a tooth to it,
    The canopy of winter is nailed there, a new roominess tramps down
        silence

SPIRIT OF TIME:
    Until violence, violence, violence is here
    Like eight hundred million trucks in competition.
    In fact there is nothing, the countries unstable, place division on my soul!

MODERNITY:
    So we bought second-hand shirts, formerly rich men's neckties, thready
        golf pants, and so on;
    Will anyone understand you as you fall
    Forward into dismay?

K:

              The unanimity of humanity, I mean the fellowship
Is on a line with the unanimity of indifference. If we had only one ball
How it would bounce! Unfortunately we have hundreds of thousands.

MODERNITY:

    Gayety triumphant in the middle of small kettles
    Pockets drum aware that we can die, our legacy
    For the foods' months. Such happiness to be going straight by
    Is holiday, best for the young, for the nude in spirit
    And our unstuck sky.

K:

    I went back to Greece once after that. I spent several days in Athens,
    With my wife, Janice. I was looking for an American woman,
    A very rich woman, who, someone had told me, loved poets
    And liked to give them money. At last, I thought,
    We could get to a good party instead of sitting every day
    In Athens's main square, which was pretty agreeable in any case—
    Minuscule cups of coffee so strong it had a beard

J (A WOMAN, HIS WIFE):

    With, to the side, large sparkling glasses of water.

K:

    So we sat there
    But the rich woman did not appear. The heroine of the Greek Resistance
    Where was she, too? This was five years later.
    So much had happened. What had happened to her?

HEROINE OF THE GREEK RESISTANCE:

    A barge of sparkling shears had happened to the herd
    The whistling from the sides of the Aegean. I am a town,
    You are a princess, she is a grove
    Filled with Italy. Saint Sinus Difficulty assailed me. I went into obliquity.
    Hello, dancers. Hello, creeks. Branches of lilies.
    Is time here going to take us? take us back?

K:

                       A rat
    Moved forward, a rat leaving some tea leaves,

And I say, Un rat! to the waiter, who was promptly relieved
By several other waiters, who made quite a stir, a drama of hay-mows
And cummerbunds, winning my local bride to me
In five seconds, we leaned across, the table, torpedoed, war! I'd like
Coffee. There is no more. Adapt.
I can't stop it. Folly.
Where the wolf stops me. A dune was walking—

TIME:

Yes but you don't receive—

K:

It is an interruption
That time makes indirect—

SPIRIT OF TIME:

Or direct, in Babylon, years ago—

J, AS THE HEROINE OF THE GREEK RESISTANCE:
The sharpness clears the bay.

END

EDWARD
AND
CHRISTINE

A NOTE ON THIS PLAY

The two main characters are EDWARD *and* CHRISTINE. *They appear sometimes as themselves, sometimes in the guise of other characters. For example, in the last Egyptian scene,* CHRISTINE *is* HATHOR; *in the Libreville scene,* EDWARD *is* HERVE BLANC, CHRISTINE *is the* CASINO GIRL. *This is all indicated in the text.* EDWARD *and* CHRISTINE *appear in diverse and rapidly changing scenes that aren't continuous in the ordinary sense of the word: a scene in one country is followed by a scene in another which is at an earlier or later time. There are big spaces between the scenes, but these spaces are skipped; the play goes from one to the other. This movement from scene to scene is not meant to be ironic; the movement and the resulting fragmentation are meant, rather, to be a sort of representation of what experience is actually like when it is free from, though not ignoring, the needs and conventions of the moment and the continuity they usually impose. I mean to put experiences together the way memory and passion and reflection do and to present the result as ordinary reality so as to make it visible.*

CRETE

(*A hillside.* EDWARD *climbs the hill, looks down the other side and sees a* GIRL, *about 12 years old, who is tending sheep.*)

EDWARD:
Ah . . . hello, there! Hello!?

GIRL:
Hel- lo. I- love you!

EDWARD:
Well, I love you, too! You're beautiful. You with your sheep. This little promontory. I up here, you down there. "I love you". Where did you learn to say that? What soldier or tourist—? The world is at peace. It has been more or less at peace for ten years. But Greece is still suffering from the terrible, perhaps unhealable wounds of its Civil War!

(SOLDIERS *walk past.* GIRL *picks up a baby lamb and shows it to* EDWARD)

GIRL:
I love you.

HYDRA

FILMMAKER (*entering*):
How can it (film-making) compare to anything
Inscribed in language or in stone? Theatre on the other hand is all
motion

And language inscribed on motion. Film is a dead hand
Placed on the living shoulder of a sex goddess such as Monroe
Or Cathleen ni Houlihan, the personification of Ireland.
I come to bring snow
That will vanish in the tracks of the sun. My movie, *Agorokoritso,*
    concerns a young lady
Who is, as the title suggests, a tomboy; eventually, however, she becomes
    a more conventional girl,
She meets the "right" Greek boy and finds "love." Then the movie is
    over. Now my work is done.
Shall I start to do another of these totally useless œuvres?
Or yet perhaps not totally useless! I see a young man and woman coming
Who apparently were impressed by my film.

EDWARD:

                                        If that isn't the worst movie

CHRISTINE:

    We've ever seen

EDWARD:

                      You don't know what is

CHRISTINE:

    Nor you, either!

(*They laugh and embrace.*)
(*The* FILM MAKER *strikes his hand against his head and goes off. As he leaves he speaks.*)
FILM MAKER:
    They will remember it, all the same!

EDWARD:
    Here on the way down from the movie theatre
    Are these two rabbits frozen into a stone
    Rabbit position—thinking that they can't be seen
    Unless they move—an idea rabbits have!

FIRST RABBIT:
>Hold still.

SECOND RABBIT:
>I am holding
>Absolutely still.

FIRST RABBIT:
>It is still not still enough.

SECOND RABBIT:
>Yes. I am absolutely totally
>Still.

FIRST RABBIT:
>But to me
>You seem to be
>Moving.

SECOND RABBIT:
>That is because your eyes are not still.

FIRST RABBIT:
>Go to hell.

SECOND RABBIT:
>Rabbits have no hell.
>Only the jaw of the wolf
>The fox
>Or the man.

FIRST RABBIT:
>Go to man then.

SECOND RABBIT:
>I will
>Not.

FIRST RABBIT:
>Shall we make
>Up?

SECOND RABBIT:
  Yes.

FIRST RABBIT:
  Farewell
  Friend, lover. We did quarrel for a while

SECOND RABBIT:
  But it was only a moment
  It was

FIRST RABBIT:
  Only a moment. Hist, now. Freeze!

(*Enter* CHARLEMUTH, EDWARD, *etc.*)

D E L F T

CHARLEMUTH (*a French poet*):
  The Dutch have no sense of the tragic.

EDWARD:
  Look at them happily riding their bicycles all around!

MICHEL (*also a French poet, arriving on a bike*):
  Come! I've just procured tickets for the latest Dutch tragedy, Meeinheer von Plutsch. It is the latest in a successful series of Dutch tragedies being performed at the Renaissancer Hus. Tonight at eight p.m.

EDWARD:
  So off we go to see it, a Dutch tragedy.

CHARLEMUTH:
  The Dutch have no sense of the tragic, even in the theatre.

CHRISTINE:
  I want to be married. I want to marry you, I love you, have children, the whole lot.

EDWARD:

I love you, too, but—I don't know, I don't want
To get married—
(*pause*)
I lost her. She has gone to someone else.
Charlemuth, though, and Michel are still around.

MICHEL:

Ha ha ha ha, ho ho ho ho, har hah who hah.

CHARLEMUTH:

Ah! les hollandais!

PARIS

(*Snow falls. A small hotel room.*)

EDWARD:

To sleep. Perchance to dream. . . . (*he sleeps*)

MOTHER:

ED ward! This is your mother!

FATHER (*shaking the door*):

Edward! Get up! What are you doing? This is your father!

EDWARD:

Huh? Huh? What?

(*He leaps out of bed*)

I am up! And they're not here! I would take a walk in the snow, in the just
early falling snow, but a peculiarity of this hotel on the rue de Fleurus is
that after ten o'clock at night you can get into it but you can't get out of it.
Once one is in it one is in it for the night. In this respect being here is like
being a child.

(*Enter a* GORILLA.)

EDWARD:

My God. He's scarier than my mother and father combined.

GORILLA:

Kawabata committed suicide.

EDWARD:

I am too young to have known his work and too young for this to have happened.

GORILLA:

You will see that it will happen in time.

EDWARD:

Why, then, if not my mother and father, who are you?

GORILLA:

I am far from being your mother and father.
I will bring you Ekaterina.
And now, I will give you these lines
For inspiration before you go to sleep. Kawabata said
The greatest happiness in life is drinking a scotch and soda
On the terrace of the Tokyo Hilton Hotel.

EDWARD:

What's wrong with that?

GORILLA:

Nothing. I see you may do well. Now get back to sleep.

FLORENCE

CHRISTINE:

I was afraid someone would pinch my ass.
It was windy, the street corner.

EDWARD:

We were in a country
Where they pinched it,
Played soccer
Which they took very seriously

And ass-pinching seriously.
I could have prevented that.

CHRISTINE:

I don't know how.
They're very very fast.
A man is going by, apparently innocently, just
Strolling along, he gets closer to you, you
Don't, why should you, pay any attention, he
Is reading a newspaper as he goes, or glancing
In another direction and then
Suddenly he goes—straight—

BACK IN PARIS

EDWARD (*rising in a burst of ecstatic inspiration*):

These are the Gorilla-given lines:
"Oh what a physical effect it has on me
To dive forever into the light blue sea
Of your acquaintance! Ah, but dearest friends,
Like forms, are finished, as life has ends!"

GORILLA:

Mystery! (*He now dissolves into white bright snow out the window above and falling on the Paris streets*)

EDWARD:

But what has this to do with ME? Maybe nothing. That would be good, for a change!

(*He goes to the window and looks out*)
(A CHILD, TOMMY, *enters and takes his hand. Then* TOMMY *leaves.*)

CHRISTINE:

I felt the excitement of a walk of which I didn't know the end! Adventure, Wandering! How could I not go everywhere I could?

EDWARD:

How could I not, too?

(*These two embrace.*)

EDWARD:
> I like this little house.

CHRISTINE:
> It's not so little! Yes, I do too. Look, it has this nice fireplace. And a room
> for you to work!

EDWARD:
> And a room for you to work.

CHRISTINE:
> And a little room for the baby.

EDWARD:
> And there will be space also for the new baby
> And look at the flowers outside

CHRISTINE:
> Look at the fruit trees outside!

GIANNI POGGI:
> Io sono Gianni Poggi. Sono tenore.
> Canto a l'opera lirica di Firenze abastanza spesso.
> Venite vedermi! (*sings*)
> > Venite verdermi! Ay, mi!

(*He collapses, as if dead.*)

GIANNI POGGI (*singing*):
> Addio diletta America!

CHRISTINE:
> Un Ballo in Maschera!

EDWARD:
> It's inevitable that we found this house. It couldn't be avoided.

CHRISTINE:

> Do you remember our trip here on the train?

GIANNI POGGI: (*expires*)

> Ay, mi! Addio!

RAILWAY STATION AT CHIANCIANO TERME

EDWARD:

> Let's see if I can find some food on the platform.

CHRISTINE:

> I'd like something to drink. Would you?

EDWARD:

> Yes! But there is nothing! There is ever nothing
> On these railway platforms that we see!

CHRISTINE:

> Only the green trees nodding overhead in the light
> Of the station and of the sun. Les réverbères . . . !
> Do you hear the next train coming?

EDWARD:

> Yes.

BACK IN FLORENCE

CHRISTINE:

> We were swept off.

EDWARD:

> The train station has vanished.

CHRISTINE:

> And we have this house, it's true!

GIANNI POGGI (*getting up; he was not really dead but feigning death as in an opera.*):

> Many times I have restaurant, many times I have cab,

Many times I have simple, cold stone light upon slab,
Many times I will sing, and have sung, again

CHRISTINE:

Every time at the opera, we see him—
Gianni Poggi, who has become all heroes and all tragic singing men.

EDWARD:

I liked the idea of seeing the city first
You wanted to get us settled right away.

CHRISTINE:

Well, we do have a baby sixteen months old!

A HOTEL GARDEN IN TAORMINA

EDWARD:

We've just seen another Antonello
Da Messina.

CHRISTINE:

                    In a little ruined
Chapel, five miles from here.
Whew! We're worn out!

EDWARD'S MOTHER:

Edward, where is Melissa? I want her to come with me
To the hairdresser's.

EDWARD'S FATHER:

This young man that we met on the train
I think he's peculiar Edward can you imagine that
He wanted me to buy him jeans in exchange for his sexual favors.

POPULACE:

Etna is erupting!

MOTHER:

From here it is very hard to see the beach.

EDWARD:

> My mother with her hat on,
> My father with the Eternal Cigarette

ANTONELLO DA MESSINA:

> I am Antonello da Messina
> Now I live in catalogues and in the sky—
> With my beloved Madonna

EDWARD:

> Do you see the way the Virgin is sitting and regarding
> The viewer? This man introduced easel painting into Italy.
> He found it in Holland and in Flanders. Before that
> All painting was on wood or on walls. Where could it have gone,
> That wall-dependent art? Antonello ruined painting, An-
> Tonello saved painting.

MOTHER:

> Edward! Oooh, you don't know what it's like to
> get old!

ANTONELLO:

> Never again the horse face
> Never again the dew. Congratulations
> On your forthcoming wedding ceremony!

EDWARD & CHRISTINE:

> We're already married!

CRETE

NYMPHS:

> Every day before full sunrise we come
> To renew ourselves at this altar,
> The Altar of the Nymphs! Everyone thinks we are gone
> Forever! But we live on
> As long as there is water or air for us
> At this marble-fountained altar!

(KATIE & BUDDY *are coming up the hill on which the Altar of the Nymphs stands*)

BUDDY:

> Aw, it's too steep! Why are we dragging ourselves all the way up here? I don't want to. I want to get back down.

KATIE:

> Come on, Buddy. It's supposed to be very interesting. And now it's just a little way.

BUDDY:

> We've already come a long way
> It's always just a little way more.

KATIE:

> Well, we got here. There! Look at it!

BUDDY:

> Wow! Okay, let's go down.

KATIE:

> You're impossible. Wait for me. I'm going over here to look
> At this what seems to be the remains of a statue. I can see a face!

BUDDY:

> So long!

(*He leaves*)

KATIE:

> It really was a carving. Of a nymph here. Buddy!
> Buddy! Where have you gone?
> (*The* NYMPHS, *who became invisible when the two persons appeared, are still audible. Now they laugh a silvery laughter.*)
> And that noise! Buddy, Buddy, where are you?
> (KATIE *wanders around in search of* BUDDY. *The light changes from morning to afternoon to dusk to dark.* KATIE *is now at home.*)

FATHER:

> Where is your brother?

KATIE:

> Oh god, I don't know!

(BROTHER *comes in—very late and a bit happiness-sodden.*)

FATHER & MOTHER:
Buddy! Where were you? How could you do that, stay out so long?

BUDDY:
I met a girl.

KATIE:
I know that the girl was not I
For I am the one who was with him at the Altar of the Nymphs
When he "disappeared"—

MOTHER:
Mussolini, who controlled Rhodes for twenty years, did some good
things.
He made the trains run on time. If he were here, Buddy would have soon
come home.

BUDDY (*displeased by his mother's political views*):
I'm going out again.

FATHER:
No. You're NOT!

(FATHER *becomes* MUSSOLINI *and keeps* BUDDY *in.*)

FLORENCE

(*Enter* EDWARD, *very distraught.*)

EDWARD:
My wife is dying! She has hemorrhaged and she needs blood.
I'm told that there is no blood and that there is no one no one in the
hospital
Who can come and help me find some. But my wife needs it
Or she'll die! Doctor, I beg you! Please!

DOCTOR:
Yes, I will go with you.
I think it is worth it. I think I can help you to find this blood.

Do you know there is a shortage? Because of Hungary? the attempted
  rebellion
Against the Russians? We're going to have a hard time.

(DOCTOR *goes with* EDWARD *to a blood supply station.*)
  Signora, we need a vial of Rh Negative Blood. Di sangue air akka
    negativo.

OLD WOMAN:
  But there is none. Here, take this!

EDWARD:
  Regard it! It is positive.

DOCTOR:
  It is not negative. It is positive! E positivo!

OLD WOMAN:
  Like everything that breathes and lives
  It is both negative and positive at the same time.

DOCTOR:
  Old woman, we want, not philosophy, but blood. Give us some negative.

OLD WOMAN:
  There is only one vial left.
  The rest has been sent to Hungary
  To give to the wounded!

DOCTOR:
  Give it to us!

EDWARD:
  How reluctantly she does so!

(*Back in the hospital*)

  And now she has it
  And she revives.

CHRISTINE:
  I'm— I'm better..

EDWARD:

But you could die!

PARIS

EDWARD (*in bed*):

Tell me that you're not gay.

CHRISTINE (*in bed*):

That's ridiculous. I have been your mistress and your wife. Then we were divorced. Why would I still be sleeping with you if I were gay?

EDWARD:

I thought you wouldn't even bother to ask me that.

CHRISTINE:

You ARE ridiculous.

EDWARD:

If I am so ridiculous why have you come back to me? why are you in bed with me? why did we make love? Will we ever have any self-understanding at all?

CHRISTINE:

Some people are not like others. I am not like you.
I find you—detestable. Go to sleep.

EDWARD:

Go to sleep? How can I? I can't possibly go to sleep now.

(*They sleep. Morning. They are up.*)

CHRISTINE (*she is making the bed*):
I detest him.

EDWARD (*he is making coffee*):
She is loathsome.

CHRISTINE (*as she drinks some coffee*):
He is a horror

EDWARD (*breakfast over*):
   I want to go to the movies today

CHRISTINE:
   Let's go then.

(*She takes his hand as they go out. She says, quietly*):
   Phhhhhhhtff!
(*They leave, then come back*)

EDWARD:
   Hurry. Alfred is coming to dinner. I have a libretto I want to show him. I'm still writing it.

CHRISTINE:
   I'm hurrying!
   Ah, hurry!
   Unsatisfying as a traffic jam!
   Like the slam
   Of a steel and iron door! Shazam!

EDWARD:
   This libretto of tentacles of ice
   This libretto of license and fright
   This libretto of leaves!
   O Paradise
   That a creator feels!
   But am I really a creator?
   Maybe I am just an automobile without wheels
   And maybe some benumbed Henry Ford was my creator
   Or maybe I am—but now the south wind steals
   In scriggle scraggle lace across my brow—
(*He writes*)

(ALFRED *arrives at the door, is shown in, sits down.*)

ALFRED:
   It's very beautiful of course
   But I don't think it will go over in France
   Why doesn't they don't she and he
   Make love even one time
   Despite their doubt?

206

EDWARD:

But he thinks he may be her father.

ALFRED:

So—I still think the French would find it incredible that they didn't even make love once, since they don't really *know* if they're related.

EDWARD:

Oh you've been living over here too long, is what!

CHRISTINE:

Edward wanted their break-up to seem a necessary thing. This is what happens in the libretto. A young married couple Bert and Matilda their car breaks down in the desert and the only one who can fix it is Henry, an "older" fellow and he has a gas station and repair shop in the middle of the desert. He and Matilda fall in love but when she says something *re* her early life he has a sudden memory thinks she may be his long-lost daughter Louisa they thus are afraid, do nothing and at the end the young couple drives off. My husband thought I didn't know but I of course did know that the libretto story was a turned-about version of something that happened in his own life. He loved a woman named Ekaterina she had a husband who was fifty years old this seemed very old to them both at that time. He couldn't take her away from her husband and child and ever after he felt he had been a coward and had ruined his life. Oh! after a decade my young husband died and no one ever set his libretto. Now at last it is going to be done, with a slightly changed conclusion that brings in what really happened in his (and our) life and by a fine (though not Alfred) composer and the premiere is at the Théatre des Champs Elysées tonight and I will be there.

Whereas Ekaterina
Ekaterina is she still alive?

(HENRY—*played by* EDWARD—*&* MATILDA/LOUISA *played by* CHRISTINE—*come onstage and sing, in operatic fashion*)

HENRY (*sings*):

O! Louisa! Matilda!

MATILDA:

Ah!

EKATERINA:

I am alive and I am in New Jersey and I know nothing of this libretto nor
of this opera nor of this world premiere night.

PARIS

CHRISTINE (*as* GILBERTE):

Not knowing what to do
I walk here and there.
I continue my studies
In law. But I am restless, restless
In my limited modernity!
I feel limited, as by a wall
Of electricity by the woman and man who
Brought me into the world and brought me up!
I stammer when I'm with them. Sometimes
I want to kill myself I
Am amused by the young American
I see everyday at the Crèmerie
De Luxembourg. Here he is now.

EDWARD:

Gilberte! Ha ha. Bonjour. Bon soir. Et cetera.
Ha ho. Wouldst thee likes to taking walk?

CHRISTINE:

You don't speak French
Perfectly yet but it is nice
To talk to you and to walk
With you, but I
Have depressing ideas, les idées noires.
I do not think that it is best that I go on seeing you. Good-bye!

(*She goes.*)

EDWARD:

Gilberte! my evening star! my hope!
I'll follow you!

208

Oh, nonsense! Damn! I'm lonely but I don't
love Gilberte! I love her name
I read about her every day
In Proust—

CHRISTINE (*a little ways off, listening*):
I can't—no matter how he feels.

L U X O R

It's the Temple of Luxor!

EDWARD:
I enter the Temple and I'm crying. Why?

(*Silence*)

Because you're going to leave me
And it reminds me of your legs.

CHRISTINE:
What does?

EDWARD:
This Temple does, its columns.
Its columns remind me of your strong and beautiful legs.
And you're going to leave me.
Its columns remind me of your legs. This Temple does.

CHRISTINE:
You came here without me and without the guide.

EDWARD:
And YOU will go off with someone not me.
These columns remind me of your legs.
The way you would put one of them over me
In the morning, when I couldn't sleep.

CHRISTINE:
The boat starts moving again.

EDWARD:

 Wait, I'm coming along.

KENYA

(EDWARD *and* CHRISTINE *go off and come riding in on* ELEPHANTS. *Each dismounts, stands beside an elephant and speaks for it.*)

ELEPHANT (EDWARD):

 The savanna is good and hot. And it is bad and hot. But the good thing is
  that it is full of trees.
 Oh impossible even to imagine, for an elephant, a tree-less savanna!

SECOND ELEPHANT (CHRISTINE):

 These wombs would cease
 To bear, on a savanna without trees.

FIRST ELEPHANT (EDWARD):

 We need the savannah
 And the savanna, to control its trees, needs us. We smack at them as at
  the keys
 Of a grand piano and we rend them more than a gigantic rat would
  cheese
 And we do not worry much about other residents of the savanna—

(*A* LION *enters and looks around curiously*)

SECOND ELEPHANT (CHRISTINE):

 Except for this one
 He *could* connect us to the rest of the savanna by the "food chain"—
 But he does not. No animal can eat us and we can eat none. The lion
  cannot
 Kill us. Our weight, our hide, our tusks
 Out-animal that dastard lion, pure bastard thing. But he is, though,
  dangerous,
 To baby elephants, to them alone.

(*Enter more* LIONS)

FIRST ELEPHANT (EDWARD):

 So we surround our children

(*This is acted out*)

SECOND ELEPHANT (CHRISTINE):
>   We elephants surround the baby elephants—they prance along
>   And do not know the danger of the lions we prevent
>   Until they are adult elephants themselves.
>   Then *they* can fight the lions
>   And they give birth or help give birth to elephants, themselves!

(LIONS *roar, charge, and are driven back*)

THE GREEK ISLAND OF HYDRA

(EVAN, *with friends, near the harbor*)

EDWARD *as* EVAN:
>   Don't expect ANYTHING!

(*A* WOMAN *comes up to* EVAN. *He lights her cigarette and talks and gestures to her, puts his hands on her shoulders and smiles.*)

FIRST MAN:
>   Evan is lighting a woman's cigarette. He wants her to be completely
>   understanding of and completely generous to him.
>   Then he will reward her with the Food of the Gods:

SECOND MAN:
>   Silence, talk, no children, love, and a bemused and vague infidelity.

WOMAN:
>   I want something more!

FIRST MAN:
>   Most of what Evan says can be understood in the light of this situation.

EVAN (*to the* MEN):
>   Good!

EVAN (*to the* WOMEN):
>   Enjoy it!

EVAN (*at fifty*):
　　You know, there's not so much time!

(*A* WOMAN *walks by.* EVAN *is now either 90 years old or a deaths-head skeleton.*)

EVAN (*to the* WOMAN):
　　Hello, Angel!

ELSEWHERE ON HYDRA

CHRISTINE:
　　On the porch of the hotel they sat and looked out at things they could see. They played a game. The father said, It is red but stippled, and they had to guess what it was. No that could not have been the game.

EDWARD:
　　I was sitting in an automobile four years later thinking about that game. Perhaps it was this: the mother said: I see three things beginning with an L.

CHRISTINE:
　　I meant of course in English not in Greek.

EDWARD:
　　Maybe that was possible.

CHRISTINE:
　　The child, a little girl, was at a certain disadvantage in being only five years old. She played along though, and of course the mother and the father made it easy. It was best when she would win. After they played the game for about half an hour, the mother took the child inside.

EDWARD:
　　Their rooms were on long corridors. Bathrooms were at the far, non-porch end. After a while the father got up and went in to his room. The mother (she was thirty-one) was lying in the bed. The father was thirty-six. He looked fondly at her and said, Did you like the game?

CHRISTINE:
　　I lied Yes. Then I said, I'm asleep.

GABON—LIBREVILLE

EDWARD *as* HERVÉ BLANC:
> I hate to leave Millie, but I have to go back
> Unless it is my whole life that I want to spend here in Gabon.
> My life isn't moving, isn't going anywhere here.

CHRISTINE *as* GABON CASINO GIRL (*blonde and British*):
> Hervé's going back troubles me
> He has a girlfriend, Millie, here. I don't think he'll take her to France.

EDWARD *as* HERVÉ BLANC:
> I don't see how I can take her
> I have to be there myself first.
> Maybe she'll never come . . . Oh
> Sweet paradise of early hotel morning—
> Stamp too big to go on the postcard, I must away—
> Large breasts of this Gabonese morning, this earth, this hotel—

CHRISTINE *as* CASINO GIRL:
> Hervé's gone.

MILLIE (*sitting, elsewhere in Libreville*):
> Hervé is leaving, as I always knew he would.

CHRISTINE *as* CASINO GIRL:
> Could you give me my glasses, please?

HER BEDMATE (MAN) (*he gives her her glasses and also puts on his own as if to see what is happening, then takes them off*):
> Let's go back to sleep.

(*Sound of steamship leaving*)

ITALIAN-FRENCH FRONTIER—DOMODOSOLLA NEAR NICE

CHRISTINE:
> Edward, give me the baby—
> Or should I take out the bags?
> Here's French Customs!

(*It is very dusty and extremely* HOT)

FRENCH CUSTOMS PERSON (FEMALE):
> Quel cauchemar! What a nightmare
> To travel with a new-born child!

EDWARD:
> The day is mild. And yet I see a sort of promised zoo
> Of clouds, in the sky.

CHRISTINE:
> Yes, I do too!

FRENCH CUSTOMS PERSON:
> I'd suggest that you get out of here fast!

CHRISTINE:
> But what did we do?

FRENCH CUSTOMS PERSON:
> Nothing! But it will be hard for you
> Travelling with this baby!

EDWARD:
> It doesn't matter, dear what we have done.
> It is what we WILL do in all this time to come!
> And live in the bright confusion
> Of extreme life!

ITALIAN CUSTOMS PERSON (MALE):
> Come! Come! We admire your baby
> Here there is nothing and really there is nothing
> But dust and butterflies and mainly only dust. But such a lovely baby!
> But let's now for the moment see
> If you are transporting drugs or have too much or too little money.

EDWARD:
> Doesn't everyone have too much or too little money?

ITALIAN CUSTOMS PERSON (*impressed*):
> Pass—free!

EDWARD:

Thank you.

TOKYO

KAWABATA:

For me happiness is being here, sitting on the terrace of the Tokyo Hilton Hotel, drinking a Scotch and soda.

JOURNALIST:

But, Master, you have done so much work—so deep, so terrifying, so moving, so artistic and profound! How can a mere glass of scotch water be anything to that? How could not that outpace this in a second moment? Answer that.

KAWABATA:

Actually, there is no need to. Sitting here on the terrace of the Hilton is happiness itself. And in happiness, one need not speak. It is not necessary. That is what is so happy about it.

JOURNALIST:

I am sure, then, though, that there is more to it in back of this momentary feeling. This can't be happiness itself.

KAWABATA:

Happiness is only itself. Behind of course are years of work. Hard years of work. And relations with other people and with the world. But these were not happiness. Happiness is in the vigor of this malt, on this terrace of the Hilton, now!

PARIS

EDWARD *as* PAUNAMAN:

It's the worst kind of weather for writing poetry—cold, clear, and still. No snow, no rain, no wind, even. Just sun but cold. Extremely cold. In which clarity, such freezing clarity, I don't feel moved to write.

A VOICE (CHRISTINE):

Be moved to write!

PAUNAMAN:

Ah, now, I am moved to write! I feel SOMEthing. It is beginning to happen. If often starts this way, a poem. What will it be about?

A VOICE:

Write it and see.

PAUNAMAN:

The breeze
Of inspiration! Indeed, *le souffle!*

(WIND *blows papers hectically all about. After the wind stops,* PAUNAMAN *stoops down to pick up the various wind-blown pages.*)

PAUNAMAN:

It's finished! I'll call it "The Lockets". I wonder if it's any good?

GABON—LAMBARÉNÉ

EDWARD *as* DOCTOR:

Albert Schweitzer's Hospital!
His celebrated clinic in Lambaréné. Lambaréné
May I be worthy of my great forebear
Albert Schweitzer! May I find the secret of clinical medicine at this Lambaréné
And, perhaps more important, Schweitzer's secret of the worship of life—
To kill even a mosquito was a heavy crime to him. Then, even a bacterium? a germ? a virus?
How does Schweitzer cure, with this absurd respect for "Life"—I mean, of course, all kinds of life?
For it is always one kind of life that kills another. Always so.

(*Panoramic stage-filling perhaps even theater-filling scene of birds killing insects, eagles killing birds, men shooting eagles, lions killing zebras, and so on. In the midst of all this the* DOCTOR *walks toward the Clinic. Suddenly, several* M'PONGWE *run out, surround, and kill him.*)

DRIVER:

What? What have you done? You crazy cannibals!
Why did you kill this man?

M'PONGWE:

>We are not cannibals—
>Unlike the Fang, the main tribe that inhabits Gabon.

OTHER M'PONGWE:

>No. We are not.

PARIS

CHRISTINE *as* DENISE:

>Here we are, three young women.

ANGELINE:

>Standing in front of great Notre Dame Monument, Queen of the Day
>>and of the Night.

NORA:

>I am blind, but I do love its each detail!

CHRISTINE *as* DENISE:

>Nora, let me put your hand here. This is
>The left side of the right-hand portal. These
>Are the spare, elongated, utterly spiritualized stone
>Figures of Christ his father his mother and the Saints.
>They are supposed to be the most beautiful of all.

ANGELINE:

>With no excess decoration. No disturbing gesture. No
>Concern for any style but spirit in stone.

NORA:

>Oh!

CHRISTINE *as* DENISE:

>I am in the midst of a destructive relationship
>With a man, a doctor, rich, arrogant, unfaithful even to me
>He has just gone to Gabon with another woman—

ANGELINE:

>I have always felt that women did not feel overt sexual desire.
>This idea is absurd but I seem stuck with it. When I have sexual desires

I feel that I am less a woman. I am chagrined. I want to deny I have them—
But then I am so surprised by them
Sometimes, that I give in, sexually,
To the most inappropriate men. And about this I can say nothing
Even to these two who are my friends. When I speak of it, they don't hear
    me.
Ah, how much Nora
Enjoys this cathedral!
More than I ever did, or could, even. I know it.

DENISE:

Yes. She does. Nora! You seem to like Notre Dame so much!

NORA:

Well, I do. Shall we go inside?

KENYA—NAIROBI

(*A hotel room*)

CHRISTINE:

He closed the university down.

EDWARD:

Who did?

CHRISTINE:

Mobutu did. So I may never see my boy friend again.

EDWARD:

I am your boy friend.

CHRISTINE:

No. Not quite. I don't know you.

EDWARD:

But here we are alone in this Kenyan hotel.

CHRISTINE:

You forgot the reason I came to your hotel.
It was not to make love to you

But to clean up. There isn't a bath in mine. It's not so nice as this.
Don't you remember?

EDWARD:
I remember all the time in which we have not made love, our entire life.

CHRISTINE:
Maybe all right, but maybe not all right.

EDWARD:
What does that mean?

CHRISTINE:
It means maybe I will—
But meanwhile tell me about yourself. Are you married?

EDWARD:
Tell me about your Peace Corps life.

CHRISTINE:
It is identical with my life, with all my life.
My entire life is like an assignment to the Peace Corps.
I'll make love to you.

(*Lights out then back on. Many coins—pennies, dimes, and nickels—shower to the floor*)

EDWARD:
Look! the future and the past! I'll go and pick them up.

(*He gets out of bed and starts to pick up the coins.*)

CHRISTINE (*rising on one elbow*):
So now no classes for a while!

VENICE—THE LAGOON

(JULIAN *and* MADDALO, *landing on a beach with their gondola*)

EDWARD *as* JULIAN:
Let me tell you, Maddalo,

As in this your gondola
We float languidly in this lagoon,
Christianity is like an island
Upon which lives a madman
Who claims he died of love.
But it is not true that he died of love!
He died the way we all died, Maddalo.
Whoever cannot see this is a madman,
And should be, straight, ejected from this gondola! (*He laughs*)

CHRISTINE *as* MADDALO:

Julian, lift your eyes and see this island
Locked into the blue mist of this lagoon—
There is none like it, else, in this lagoon!
Upon it lives a man made mad by love
Who lives his life sequestered on this island.
As certain as my name is Maddalo
I longed to see him and have steered my gondola
This way, to have some words with this said "madman"!
Are you the madman?
I think that you are not! I am Maddalo
And this is Julian.

MADMAN:

I, in this lagoon,
Have seen no one for seven years. For love—
When my Maria died—I broke my gondola
And yours is the first sign of any gondola
I've seen in all this time upon my island!
Be welcome here!

MADDALO:

We thank you. But, come back
With us, dear lover, and be nursed to health!

JULIAN:

Yes, with us to the sheltered mainland come,
Where bonny nurses will amend your state
Of being, till you shine with life again!

MADMAN:

> Alas, too late! You are kind my Lords, but one was kinder still,
> And she is dead. And now I too must die. Farewell.

(*He falls down dead*)

FLORENCE

DOCTOR:

> We'll have to get more blood. But there is none in Florence.

EDWARD:

> What will we do then?

DOCTOR:

> There is a convent hospital across the river, ten kilometers away. They may have some there. (*They drive there and enter the hospital.*) I can't disturb the Sister—a service is going on. She has the key.

EDWARD:

> The key to the place where the blood is stored?

DOCTOR:

> Yes.

EDWARD:

> Disturb her. It IS a matter of life and death.

DOCTOR:

> All right. Mille scusi, suora, ma abbiamo bisogna—c'io e sarebbe possibile avere un fiasco di sangue air akka negativo.

NUN:

> Certo. Buona sera signori.

EDWARD:

> Buona sera, grazie!

CHRISTINE:

They came and told me I had to choose a name for the baby.
Otherwise they couldn't bury it. You know, I'm afraid!
I'm mostly afraid I won't be able to love Molly.
I've had for so long the idea of the other baby with her, all the time.
And now that he's—not here—I'm not sure I can love her.

EDWARD:

I know you will. I'll help you.

PROVENCE

(*Cherry trees are quarrelling—voices of waving branches*)

BLOSSOMING CHERRY TREE:

Admire me. That's my due, I am
More beautiful than you.

SECOND BLOSSOMING CHERRY TREE:

You can't see yourself. So it's impossible for you to know.
But I see you. And I tell you that it isn't so.

FIRST BLOSSOMING CHERRY TREE:

What you say makes no sense.

SECOND BLOSSOMING CHERRY TREE:

It makes sense.

FIRST BLOSSOMING CHERRY TREE:

Makes no sense. I am more beautiful than you.

SECOND BLOSSOMING CHERRY TREE:

Absurd cherry!

FIRST BLOSSOMING CHERRY TREE:

Stupid, very!

SECOND BLOSSOMING CHERRY TREE:

Frowzy boughs!

FIRST BLOSSOMING CHERRY TREE:
> Secondary!

SECOND BLOSSOMING CHERRY TREE:
> Evening goes its rounds
> With darks to not see you!

FIRST BLOSSOMING CHERRY TREE:
> You are a fireman's shoe!

SECOND BLOSSOMING CHERRY TREE:
> It is I who am more beautiful than you.
> See how the sun shines through.

FIRST BLOSSOMING CHERRY TREE:
> It is shining on me
> O deluded cherry tree!

SECOND BLOSSOMING CHERRY TREE:
> YOU are the deluded tree! . . .

CHRISTINE:
> Oh, what I have been through,
> I hate quarreling, gone through!
> Blossoming cherry trees, even,
> Fight. That's terrible—for them, for me.

EDWARD *as* DIETRICH (*standing by his boat*):
> Come, can you go out with me?

CHRISTINE:
> I don't want to quarrel,
> Dietrich.

EDWARD *as* DIETRICH:
> I don't—quarrel?—understand. Will
> You come or no?

CHRISTINE:
> Oh, Yes!

(*She turns lightly then speaks again as if to answer herself.*)

CHRISTINE:
> No!

ZAIRE—OUTSKIRTS OF KINSHASA

ANNOUNCER:
> Ladies and Gentlemen, Achille Dogos! Achille Dogos presents
> *Leaders of the Wartime and Post-War World!*

(*In the middle of the* BUSH, *in a cleared space,* ACHILLE DOGOS, *puts on a play:* LEADERS OF THE WAR-TIME AND POST-WAR WORLD. DOGOS *takes on the characters of the main leaders of Europe and America from about 1939 to 1980. Very little of what he says (often sings, shouts, screams, or whispers) can be heard. What can be heard most clearly are the transitional phrases spoken at the introduction of each new personage, transitions accomplished always by means of* PUNS, *which should be rather heavily emphasized.*)

ACHILLE DOGOS (*as* ROOSEVELT):
> Hey ha ha! Where you build a church? It's up on a hill, that's why we call it CHURCH HILL!

(DOGOS *feigns entrance as* WINSTON CHURCHILL)

ACHILLE DOGOS (*as* CHURCHILL):
> Did I hear my name? Going to strike the animal, strike it where it sleeps. We have to HIT LAIR! Ho, ho, speak!

(DOGOS *feigns entrance as* ADOLF HITLER)

DOGOS (*as* HITLER):
> Well I am Hit Lair! Who now says my name? If then when my friend feels not so strong, he'll lean on me. He must LEAN ON ME!

(DOGOS *feigns entrance as* BENITO MUSSOLINI)

DOGOS *as* MUSSOLINI:
> Ho, I am Benito Must-Lean-On-Me . . .

(*Finally, after much more stage action,* DOGOS *appears as* JOHN F. KENNEDY)

224

DOGOS *as* KENNEDY:
> We must have peace! . . .

(*A* SHOT. DOGOS *falls down as if dead.* SPECTATORS *scream: No! no! no! no! no! no!* DOGOS *now gets up, as himself, and bows, to great applause.*)

CHRISTINE *as* SERAFINE (*tells her story as she runs along—either jogging or, perhaps preferably, really running to get to or away from something or someone; occasionally, she seems a little out of breath*):
> I had a, well, a thing with a very important man . . . An industrialist. Lived in Zaire. We were. It was a man of fifty-eight years. I was sixteen. We were happy. Last year he had a massive heart attack. He was not quite dead but the affair was over. He was enfeebled, weak to the point of bed rid. He cannot move his arm.

EDWARD *as* THE INDUSTRIALIST (*from offstage, loudly but haltingly*):
> Frédérique!

SERAFINE (*reaches the banks of the Congo River and gets into a pirogue*):
> But his servant does not hear and does not come because.

EDWARD:
> I am living.

SERAFINE:
> Oh but for me it is as if he is dead.

EDWARD:
> How in her pirogue she glides
> Like a flower seen from all sides!
> She the universe divides
> Into sunshine, rain and snow.

SERAFINE:
> I at sixteen still was so—La! I came like a gilded butterfly

EDWARD:
> Tell the rest.

SERAFINE (*sings*):

Mi chiamono Serafina!

Sono bella come un angelo!

Sono stata per due anni con un grand' industriale!

Lui ammalato, io partivo!

Mi chiamano Serafina. Ora, o diciotto anni!

EDWARD:

Bella istoria!

SERAFINE:

I came like a gilded butterfly to pose on the stark dark arm of the man
with two billion francs three years before he was going to die.

CHIEFTAIN:

My wife is in an elegant room taking care of me.

We French are the cleverest people in Europe. This continent is dark,
but its sun is bright.

Dying in Africa, I think of this girl.

SERAFINE (*now back on shore again, and running*):

My father was a friend of his, in the Ministry of African Affairs. He told
my father he loved me and my father told him, "If you make her happy—"
My father was really horrified, though. When he put his hand on my
father's shoulder, my father instinctively recoiled. (*She stops, out of breath*)
His heart attack finished it really. I had to leave Africa. At that point
everything was impossible! (*She runs off very fast now, headed for France.*)

GREECE/HYDRA

EDWARD *as* TERENCE, *a painter*:

I can't stop drinking. I don't even want to stop drinking. I'm going crazy.
I think perhaps I am already crazy! This island, to me, is like a hospital.
With fine medicine! More ouzo, ha ha! More wine! More beer!

CHRISTINE *as* WAITER:

Would you like something to eat with that, Poustoukis?

EDWARD *as* TERENCE:

> Poustoukis? What's that? Why do you call me that? Do you want to have a drink with me after you're off? What time would that be tonight?

CHRISTINE *as* WAITER:

> No I am sorry sir Poustoukis. I can't. But I can bring you another drink and something to eat.

EDWARD *as* TERENCE:

> Well, I'd rather have you but I'll take a beer. Bring me a piece of bread, perhaps. I don't really want anything to eat. I know that I'll be sent home crazy before long. Ah! ha ha! I'd rather have you than a beer!

(*He passes out.*)

EDWARD (*no longer* TERENCE):

> I've thought of a song.
> (*poses in a grand operatic way to sing*)
>> Black is the COVER
>> —Do you get it, it's a yarmulka—a Jewish folksong—
>> Black is the COVER of my TRUE LOVE's hair—

CHRISTINE:

> Yes, it's funny. It really is . . . Listen! Do you hear?

DROWNED SAILORS' VOICES:

>> Kale Khios! . . .
>> Kore! . . .
>> Rododaktolos Eos! . . .

(*Now* TERENCE *goes by, on a boat*)

VOICE OF TERENCE:

> O Oinops Pontos!. . . . This world, this water, are lost.

EGYPT

CHRISTINE:

> Downstairs the children are very busy on the machines.

EDWARD:

They seem to be six, seven, eight, ten years old. Weaving.

OFFICIAL:

Doing this work, the children can make money, entirely due to the kindness of you, which will eventually enable them to go to school.

CHRISTINE:

Obviously not true!
A horrible enterprise.
To give to the children is to condone it.

EDWARD:

But we can't avoid the problem like that.
Once we are here, we are here.

CHILD:

Give me please. (EDWARD *does*.) Thank you.

CHRISTINE:

Foolish.

EDWARD:

I suppose so.

CHRISTINE:

But what else can be done?

EDWARD:

Whatever. But we are not going to do it on this tour.

CHILD:

I'll work faster and faster. It was my speed and efficiency that made him give me so much!

CHRISTINE:

What did she say?

EDWARD:

Let's get on the bus! It's going. We don't want to be left here!

HAITI—PORT-AU-PRINCE, HOTEL GARDEN

CHRISTINE'S MOTHER:
> I'm very sorry—I can't tell you how sorry—that
> Moulson's turned up in this place!

CHRISTINE'S FATHER:
> He—ah, the doctor.
> Well, that's all over, isn't it? I'm sorry it's so unpleasant for you—

HAITI—COUNTRY ROAD

CHRISTINE:
> I'm lost. I never saw this road
> Drums! This is the place they were talking about, where you can hear
> Drums. On my own I found it.

(*Enter* PROCESSION OF THE DEAD, *in* MASKS)

> A procession! A parade.

(*Drums louder,* PROCESSION *nearer.*)

LEADER:
> Watch out, Little Lady, that we don't trample you down!
> Our emblem is the SNAKE,
> It goes in all directions.

(*He hurls a* SNAKE *on the stage. It rises, curls, curves, does many snakelike movements.*)

CHRISTINE (*frightened by the* SNAKE *as she was not by the* PROCESSION OF THE DEAD):
> Yikes! A cobra! I don't know what. A snake! It may be a rattler! I'm getting
> out of here!

LEADER:
> Farewell!
> Come my Dead Ones, further!

(*They march off.* CHRISTINE *approaches a cafe table off to one side where* DR. MOULSON (EDWARD) *is sitting.*)

CHRISTINE:
Uh, ah . . . Hello, Sir. Doctor Moulson?

EDWARD *as* DR. MOULSON:
Christine! What are you doing, off in this odd place?

CHRISTINE:
I wanted to hear the drums. But there's a snake over there, a really scary one! (*She lights a cigarette.*)

DR. MOULSON:
A snake? Well, I'll go see. Does your mother allow you to do that?

CHRISTINE:
No. Over there.

(MOULSON *goes, looks, and comes back.*)

DR. MOULSON:
Yes, in fact. A big one. But it slithered off.

CHRISTINE:
Oh my god. Well, thank you. I guess I'll be going home.

(CHRISTINE *returns to the hotel garden*)

CHRISTINE'S MOTHER:
Where were you Christine?

CHRISTINE:
I ran into Dr. Moulson

CHRISTINE'S MOTHER:
What were you doing with *him?*
Didn't I tell you not ever to speak to him?

CHRISTINE:

Oh not anything. I went out there where you can hear the drums. I heard them. But then I got frightened by a snake.

CHRISTINE'S FATHER:

Dr. Moulson? A snake? what in god's name is going on?

CHRISTINE:

Oh, nothing! (*She looks at her finger, sees a tobacco stain on it, and puts it in her mouth to hide it.*)

CHRISTINE'S MOTHER (*smoothing out her own long honey-blonde hair*):

Tell us the story!

KENYA—NAIROBI

CHRISTINE:

After the market, the sunlight hits our faces as we gradually work our way inside the shadowing garden doors of the hotel

EDWARD:

Can you spend the night?

CHRISTINE:

What would we do all night?

EDWARD:

Who built this hotel?

PARIS

During this great hot spell it's impossible to get coffee. It makes the café too hot. Cold drinks are almost impossible to find. People hoard beer, soda, bottled water. Only here and there, an old sailor, drunk and asleep in his boots, awakes with a terrible thirst and takes it for granted.

EGYPT

CHRISTINE *as* EGYPTIAN GUIDE:

Why does that disagreeable-seeming man keep looking at me?

EDWARD:

I want to see behind the appearance—

Behind that pleasure-giving feminine exterior is what seems to be an
ignorant young woman,

But behind that ignorant young woman is possibly something that is
worth the world!

CHRISTINE:

He will never find out, because I'm not going to be intimate with him.

I am not going to make love to him. Life is not long enough for that!

WILLIMANTIC, CONNECTICUT

EDWARD:

How idyllic, though, to be with you today sitting on the banks of the
Willimantic River, my idea and yours, a nice place to be, isn't it?

CHRISTINE:

Yes. Do you remember—?

EDWARD:

How could I forget? That you—

CHRISTINE:

That I was a "Red Cross Girl" and you were an enlisted soldier, a PFC. You
weren't allowed to go out with me, you weren't allowed even to touch me,
to take my hand.

EDWARD:

I did, though, in the jeep. You were the driver.

CHRISTINE:

I was the only one who could get a vehicle. It was nice to be out with you!

EDWARD:

Yes, though there was not much we could do. No place to go. Military
Saipan was a difficult place for a romance.

232

SAIPAN

CHRISTINE:
> Should we drive a little further?

EDWARD:
> I love you.

WILLIMANTIC

CHRISTINE:
> Can I show you some things from this book? I collect in it the things I like best that I read, mostly from poems; this whole section is about nature, this one about love.

EDWARD:
> Could you come to see me in New York?

CHRISTINE:
> No. You and I aren't fated to meet again.

KUNMING

WANG CHULI:
> On the Long March, during our rest periods, we read passages from
>> Whitman aloud.
> From The Song of Myself.

EDWARD:
> "I am he that walks with the tender and growing night"?
> Or "Smile, for your Lover comes!"?

WALT WHITMAN (*appearing on one side of the stage and reading softly*):
> I call to the earth and sea half-held by the night.
> Press close, bare-bosomed night—press close, magnetic nourishing
>> night!

WANG CHULI:
> I think we read something else.

EDWARD:

I wonder what.

CHRISTINE:

Oh you probably know.

EDWARD:

I don't. Young Li said you and I are spending an awful lot of time together. He is surprised we're not married. Or at least engaged.

CHRISTINE:

You are so much older than I am. But I would do it anyway.

EDWARD:

What?

CHRISTINE:

Marry you.

EDWARD:

Oh! Christine! That's very nice of you!

CHRISTINE:

Well, it was sort of a joke.

EDWARD:

I *am* living with someone else.

CHRISTINE:

Yes, but it's a "Long March" back to the United States!

EDWARD:

Thank you. But nonetheless, nonetheless . . . What a joy, though, sometimes, to talk to somebody!

CHRISTINE:

Yes, when we met two days ago in the hotel—

EDWARD:

It seemed so right away.
Is that how Whitman could have seemed to the Chinese marchers?

234

CHRISTINE:

You could ask Wang Chuli . . .

WANG CHULI:

I am still searching for the passages. I know it was not the beginning: "I celebrate Myself."

(WHITMAN *reappears.*)

WHITMAN:

And what I assume, you shall assume.
For every atom belonging to me as good belongs to you.

LEYTE

EDWARD:

I am here "in combat," an infantry soldier in the Philippines, on the island of Leyte, behind the lines. We stay here, in the tropical rainstorms and in the rare hits of sun, just waiting, waiting to be called to the front, and not doing much. Every day, at noon, we eat lunch. We open cans of C rations and K rations and eat. The food is horrible but it keeps us alive. And every day, after the first day, just as we do open those cans and prepare to eat, some Japanese planes fly over and open fire. We dive into trenches and foxholes; most of the time, after a few minutes, the raiders are gone. They've done no harm.

KANAMAKA (*leading a group of small planes*):
This way! Over here!

(*Explosion*)

EDWARD:
Ow! (*He screams*)

KANAMAKA:
You will die, Americans! Away!

EDWARD:

Why do they leave so soon, I wonder? I guess they don't consider us an important target. Then why bomb us at all? War is extraordinary.

Everything you hear, anything you see, anything you smell, even, can mean your death!

TOKYO

KANAMAKA:

Thank you for coming to this World Conference on Refolded Electronic Chips. Luncheon is served.

(*Loud noise as of chairs being knocked over violently on the floor above*)

EDWARD (*turns pale*):

My God! A lunchtime raid!

(*He dives down to the floor*)

OTHERS:

What's wrong with our American colleague? Are you all right?

KANAMAKA:

MY bombers! MY young life in the sun!

CRETE

EDWARD:

Our baby is walking up the steps.

CHRISTINE:

She's not quite a baby any more. Sixteen months!

EDWARD:

Are you sure she's all right?
In Knossos life can be dangerous.

CHRISTINE:

I suppose that three thousand years ago it was.
Minos was a horrible man!

EDWARD:

Look! The bare traces of a statue of Helios!

CHRISTINE:
>Cretan versions of Olympian gods—
>A horrible man! Sacrificing boys and girls every year—
>What kinds of gods are those?

HELIOS (*rising up out of a fallen stone statue*):
>Hungry ones! And now it is your turn! (*menaces them*)
>I am Helios!
>The ancientest Sun God!

EDWARD:
>Watch
>Out! Molly is falling!

(EDWARD *rushes over and catches the* BABY *before she hits the ground from the top step where she was*)

EDWARD:
>Ah! safe! Molly!

HELIOS:
>Curses! I'm defeated—
>I, the fierce monarch of the sun!
>(*He again becomes one with the fallen statue*)

EDWARD:
>I caught her!

CHRISTINE:
>Oh, now you are like a god!

PARIS

OTHER YOUNG MAN:
>He likes you almost as much as I do!

CHRISTINE:
>Well, of course! He's liked me for a long time!

OTHER YOUNG MAN:
>Well, I like HIM for that!

CHRISTINE:

Maybe you two should get together.

OTHER YOUNG MAN:

Ha!

EDWARD:

Would you like a drink?

CHRISTINE:

Yes. I would.

EDWARD:

Will you come to Barcelona?

CHRISTINE:

Of course. No one ever said I was "sweet".

EDWARD:

I forgot to say it. I love your dress.

CHRISTINE:

I don't think you should pay any attention to how I dress.

EDWARD:

Why not? You're wearing those clothes. You selected them. Maybe even you paid for them. You put them on. I didn't.

CHRISTINE:

Ha ha. I'd like you to dress me.

EDWARD:

Well, if I dress you then can I say I like your clothes?

CHRISTINE:

No!

EDWARD:

Why not?

CHRISTINE:

Because you'd have to buy them, too.

(*They embrace*)

EDWARD:

I love you.

CHRISTINE:

Don't say that. I told you not to say that.

EDWARD:

Why shouldn't I say that I love you? It's the truth. Besides it makes me feel good to say it.

CHRISTINE:

Well it doesn't make me feel good; it has always made me feel uncomfortable. I thought because you loved me you were much more likely to get me pregnant.

EDWARD:

I like you a lot.

CHRISTINE:

THAT it's all right to say!

EDWARD:

You're wearing a slow white dress.

CHRISTINE:

I'm going to have a baby—with someone else.

EDWARD:

Thank you for not having done this then.

CHRISTINE:

I—well, actually, we—almost did—

EDWARD:

> An arm, in my hotel room!

(*He picks up the phone*)

> Hello, Front Desk? Front desk of the Ramapawapinanda?
>
> A torn-off arm! . . . Well, what could they do, anyway?

(*He puts down the phone*)

> Here is a note attached to it, saying "To our Professor, from his most appreciative students at the University of Gabon."
>
> Why would my Gabonese students
>
> Give me a torn-off human arm?
>
> A torn-off human arm! (*pause*)
>
> How beautiful are the breasts of the half-naked wives and daughters of the lucky French residents of Gabon
>
> As they lie beside the swimming pool! Whereas I, a stranger to this country,
>
> Am confined to this thirtieth-story room with a bleeding arm!

(*Pause. He looks closely at the arm.*)

> But the arm's not "real". It has no odor. It's paper,
>
> Papier-maché.

(KNOCK *at the door. Enter* KABAMU, *or* CHRISTINE *as* KABAMU.)

EDWARD:

> Kabamu, I am glad to see you. Do you know anything about this arm?

KABAMU:

> Ah, I came to talk to you about that. It is a gift from your students
>
> In recognition and appreciation of what you told them about Ambrose Bierce. He is their favorite American author.
>
> He truly knows magic, magic that is real, as for us, magic is real.
>
> And as it seems to be, too, for you. They regard you as one of a handful of elect foreigners who see into the nature of things. Therefore the supreme
>
> Gift of "The Arm." To the Gabonese, this is the greatest honor
>
> Of all! Congratulations!

(*The door opens and many* GABONESE STUDENTS *come in, some—or all—in magic tribal costume*)

STUDENTS:

We congratulate you, Professor. *Abba kai-yi ta-boun!* Professor, congratulations.

EDWARD:

But I—but the—well, thank you . . .

(*They do a* CEREMONIAL DANCE *around him and then shouting loud and stepping high, depart, but not before snatching up the Arm to take it with them.*)

KABAMU (*at the door*):

Professor, Bon Voyage!

EDWARD (*looking around for the arm*):

But my Arm! . . .

KABAMU (*speaking from the door*):

It is not the Arm that has power but the absence of the Arm! The physical arm is nothing. That is why it is made of papier-maché! But the Arm, once invisible, can open the Gates of Life. And of Death!

EDWARD:

Life . . . Death . . . The pool . . . breasts . . . (*he falls asleep*)

MEXICO

(*A* CORPSE *walks across the Mexican flatlands*)

EDWARD *as* CORPSE:

I have been walking across the plain of Mexico for forty days.
I began my voyage in Mexico City and my destination is Oaxaca,
The city in which I was born. My objective is to find the drums there
That I used to play on, when I was alive—when I was a boy and a young
    man in Oaxaca.
These drums are at the Church of Santa Maria de la Soledad. I long to
    play on them. That
Has been my main wish since I died. I neither sleep nor rest nor take in
    nourishment nor look around
At what I am passing, but walk without stint to the City of Oaxaca
And to the DRUMS.

(*Sound of Drums.*)

> I hear them,
> I hear the Drums, walking.

(*Total darkness and night. Then glow of early morning*)

> Forty-one days! I believe this is my sister's house. Sister!
> Rosario! My sister!

CHRISTINE *as* SISTER (*coming to the door*):
> Juanito! Why, Juanito! It is—(*she faints. The* CORPSE *picks her up and carries her inside, where she becomes conscious again.*)

CORPSE:
> Rosario—

SISTER:
> Juanito, my Juanito—but you are dead!

CORPSE:
> Yes, but alive as a Corpse. To me this post-life has been granted. I do not think it can last long. May it last long enough for me to do what I wish: to play my Drums!

SISTER:
> So may it last, Juanito!

CORPSE:
> Sister, go to the Church
> Of the Soledad. Tell Father Benzares that I want my drums
> And that I wish to play them there.

SISTER:
> Si.

(*The interior of the Church of the Soledad.*)

BISHOP:
> The Corpse of Juanito is at the High Altar playing the Drums. The people, who at first fainted on seeing him, have now been brought back to

life, by the music. They listen, entranced. My Son, I shall stand beside you.

CHRISTINE *as* RAMONA (*the* CORPSE*'s dead* GIRLFRIEND):
   And so shall I.

BISHOP:
   Ramona, Juanito's first love! You, too, here! You who died a week after Juanito went to Mexico City, to make money for the marriage! Is it you?

RAMONA:
   It is I.

PEOPLE:
   Bishop! Find a way to save the Corpses from going back into Death! Juanito has made such beautiful music! He deserves happiness. We want him to remain alive!

BISHOP (*falls to his knees*):
   O Lord, grant this man and woman continuing life! It is so little a thing for Thee!

GOD:
   I can hear you, Bishop, and I have heard the music. I will grant these two life. Seven Years. After that, I would like Juanito to come up to Heaven and play for me. It's a long time that I've been without the blessing of that kind of sound!

BISHOP:
   I thank Thee, Lord. But, may I be bold? Lord, what are years to Thee? Couldst Thou not grant this man a true span of twenty-eight years, and the woman with him? And then take him to Thy breast?

(*Thunder.*)

GOD (*smiling*):
   Rather, to my Bandstand. Yes, so be it!

(*The* BISHOP *turns to offer the* CORPSES *life but the change has already taken place. Beside him are no Corpses but a somewhat puzzled-looking man of thirty-two*

holding a pair of batons and a nervous-looking woman of twenty-nine—in fact,
EDWARD *and* CHRISTINE)

BISHOP:
> Ah, I see. Well, play! You have been granted life!

FORMER CORPSE:
> I've played enough. Bishop, thank you! I have played enough.
> The great stamina of the Dead is no longer mine!

(*He embraces* RAMONA *and they come down from the Altar.*)

BISHOP:
> It is true, you have played for ten hours. The great stamina of the Dead is
> no longer yours. Live in happiness and in peace!

PEOPLE:
> Live in happiness and in peace!

MINSTREL:
> I know another version of this story! In Acuitlan they say the Corpse
> becomes the corpse of a lion and does acrobatic leaps. And another: in
> Cuzuno, it is the corpse only of a huge pair of feet, which dance. Ramona
> doesn't appear in these two stories. There is another one, though, in which
> she is the main one. SHE is the Corpse and she comes to the tiny village of
> Suninos, gets up on the Altar, and SINGS. God is so moved by her singing
> that He decides to revive the Heavenly Choir. In this version, Juanito is a
> minor character, who, while she is singing, appears at her side.

(*Sound of Angelic Choir, singing a "Gloria"*)

SHANGHAI

(EDWARD *and* CHRISTINE *are playing ping pong in the finals of an important
tournament*)

CHRISTINE (*as* SONG JIA):
> There! My point. Twisting low and to the side!

EDWARD (*as* DING WEI):
> THIS point is mine, a clear smack smash!

CHRISTINE:
> I made an error!

EDWARD:
> I made an error!

CHRISTINE:
> That I've now redeemed

EDWARD:
> That I've now redeemed

EDWARD *and* CHRISTINE:
> By this shot.

EDWARD:
> The score is even.

CHRISTINE:
> Twenty to twenty.

EDWARD:
> What you want to happen may happen but may not happen often enough!
> To win even one game, a constant succession of victories is needed.
> It is not like love.
> But now with the distraction of my thinking I have lost the game.
> Song Jia you have made two good, winning shots
> While I have been distractedly thinking.

CHRISTINE:
> To think about the main thing is not
> Always the way to win the game. At least I know that it is not
> In ping pong, where everything—maybe the whole destiny and outcome
>   of our life—
> Rides on each ball that we hit!

EDWARD:
> Now you will go to America and I will not . . .

CHRISTINE:

> Because of ping pong.

EDWARD:

> Even because of one mis–hit ball!

(*Dark then light*)

NAPLES

CHRISTINE:

> Rossini woke from a deep slumber and began to play the piano.

(EDWARD (*as* ROSSINI) *plays the piano*)

CHRISTINE AND OTHERS:

> Bravo! Bravo!

EDWARD *as* ROSSINI (*still playing*):

> The wheat withers in the fields. A baby is crying.

CHRISTINE:

> Of what use to us, after the opera is over, is Rossini?

EDWARD (*as* HIMSELF):

> We hear scraps of Rossini's music everywhere!

CHRISTINE:

> Springtime has come into its own! And despite everything, the child cries
> a little less.

(*Brave and glorious sounds of an opera.*)

CHRISTINE:

> At the Teatro San Carlo

EDWARD:

> We have the impression

CHRISTINE:

> Known to be false

EDWARD:

    That time has just begun!

MADAGASCAR

EDWARD *as* JACQUES RABEMANAJARA:

    But in colonizing the island of Madagascar
    The French introduced things that were good
    For the people, certainly, such as "Colonial hats" (*he puts one on*)
    And others that were chiefly to make them feel a part of France
    And thus more loyal, more connected (*he puts on a dark-blue Academy
        jacket*)
    Such as the Académie malgache, the Madagascar Academy,
    Modeled on the Académie française.
    Other things were bad.

MADAME RIBAVIABALA:

    They certainly were! How cruel, how horrible the French were
    To us, at certain times!

(*Enter a group of masked, stony-faced* FRENCH OFFICERS—*they remove their harsh masks*)

EDWARD *as* JACQUES:

    With its cruel mask of domination taken off,
    France offers, among the nations, too beautiful a face
    Not to have a choice spot
    In every free man's heart.
(*The* OFFICERS *put their masks back on and approach him, about to seize him*)
    Are these officers the presence
    France genuinely wants to have
    In Madagascar? Madagascar! graven in my soul!
(*A map of France is projected, or seen, in the distance*)
    And the whole problem is there—in the distance of France
    From us—the problem of every far-from-the-center action,
    Of every far-from-the-center place!

MME RIBAVIABALA:

    Those words of Jacques Rabemanajara are precious to us!
    But we are happy to see you—now that all that is done.
    Would you like to try our rice water?

EDWARD *as an* AMERICAN VISITOR:
>Yes. Thank you. What is that?

MME RIBAVIABALA:
>A drink of cool water, and the water has been boiled with rice.
>The rice is eaten, too, of course. The left-over water isn't thrown away
>But cooled and drunk. Do you like it?

EDWARD:
>Yes. Very much.

MME RIBAVIABALA:
>Here is my husband. Viens, Robair! This gentleman is come to lunch
>But not to raid.

MONSIEUR RIBAVIABALA:
>Madagascar is now free. Sir, you are welcome! Look at this gigantic
>cricket I've found!

MME RIBAVIABALA:
>Madagascar has the largest crickets in the world!

EDWARD:
>Thank you for everything. Good-bye.

MME RIBAVIABALA:
>Je vous en prie, monsieur! Adieu!

MONSIEUR RIBAVIABALA:
>Serviteur!

MOROCCO

EDWARD:
>Is the bus ever going to leave?

CHRISTINE:
>Well, it has to get here first. It IS hot here.
>Drink the tea. The hotter it is, the cooler it will make you, you know—
>it will make us sweat!

248

EDWARD:

There is an Italian man over there I think we know.
He was at the last stop with us—Ferra- Ferra—Ferrabonzo.

CHRISTINE:

Look at Beepie. She's asleep.

EDWARD:

There are bugs in the tea.

CHRISTINE:

Don't worry about the bugs. They won't hurt us.

EDWARD:

How can you be sure?

CHRISTINE:

Beepie, Beepie, wake up! Come, Sweetest. Daddy has to pay—and then
we'll get on the bus.

EDWARD:

It's come. The large, filthy, dark yellow, wheezing bus—
It is breathing harsh breaths in the street.

DRIVER:

Anybody for Elizir?

EDWARD:

Yes, we all are, I think.

CHRISTINE:

This bus smells of—

EDWARD:

Hashish. Let's get off! If the driver is smoking it, it's not safe.

CHRISTINE:

Yes. Let's go.

DRIVER:

Why are you leaving the bus? Are you coming on it or not?

(EDWARD *makes a sign of holding his nose and then of inhaling hashish, fingers at his lips. The* DRIVER *laughs.*)

DRIVER:
That previous passenger. He is gone now from the bus. Not me!

(*He indicates a wavering person some distance away.*)

FERRABONZO:
Are you sure?

DRIVER:
I am sure. Otherwise I can lose my license never to drive the bus my
children hungry.

EDWARD:
All right. I believe him. Thank you. Sorry. Let's get on.

DRIVER (*gets off the bus again and shouts into the empty café*):
Anyone for Elizir? Nobody else? Let's go!

MEDIEVAL ENGLAND

CHRISTINE:
I am Saint Ursula, and the task assigned to me by God is to find eleven
thousand virgins to take with me on a crusade to the Holy Land. On the
way there, we'll be set upon by pagans, enemies of the Faith, who will rape
and slaughter us. I have this foreknowledge but am obliged to set sail
anyway. The only way any of these young women can escape this fate is to
convince me she is not a virgin.

EDWARD:
How are you going to get them to do that?

CHRISTINE:
Young women of Britannia! Listen to me! God orders you to tell the truth.
Liars will go to Hell. Are you Virgins? Consider it carefully. If you are not a
virgin, that's fine—at least, it's all right. You won't go to hell for that. Only
for lying. It happens that I NEED VIRGINS for this one expedition. There may
be other expeditions with different requirements. I can envision perhaps a
"Red Light Crusade." But that is not what this one is. This one has got to be

a Virginiad, truly. So come to me if you are not a virgin, now. There will be no penalty, none. In fact, each one who now admits she is not a virgin will be given, by Saint Anselmo (EDWARD *smiles, acknowledging himself*) a box of candy. Confess! And from the burdens of deceit be free!

(ELEVEN THOUSAND YOUNG WOMEN *approach* ST. URSULA)

CHRISTINE:

May God be praised! The Expedition is cancelled! La spedizione e stata annulata. Grazie a dio! Praise without end.

EDWARD:

That's amazing!

THE LOWER RHINE

PAGANS:

God damn! Shit! Merde! Damn!
It will be a long time before such an expedition begins
Again.—Not in our lifetime!

SOUTHAMPTON, NEW YORK

EDWARD:

As an American painter
I never choose as a subject anything remotely like this—
Yet people say, sometimes, when they look at my paintings of people
That there is a great empty innocence about the people
As if they were St. Ursula, and the Virgins!

GREECE—ATHENS

CHRISTINE (*gesturing*):

Look at that beautiful Artemis statue there! On the vase. Could you buy it
    for me?

EDWARD:

Of course.

(*to* MUSEUM GIRL)

I'd like this vase.

GIRL IN MUSEUM:
>   I'll wrap it up.

EDWARD:
>   Oh I can't!
>   I can't buy the vase, I can't!
>   It costs too much.
>   I can't stand to spend the money.

CHRISTINE:
>   You mean you can't stand to THINK of spending the money; it isn't really
>   such a high price.
>   Besides, I'll pay you back as soon as I can change some money myself.

EDWARD:
>   It costs fifty five thousand drachmas.

CHRISTINE:
>   That's only four dollars!

EDWARD:
>   Here I'll buy these smaller vases
>   Tiny ones with silly prices
>   Five cents for one
>   And six for another. How
>   Can they tell the difference? I'll
>   Take four—no five—no four—no five—

NEW YORK

EDWARD:
>   My desk faces a window and on it I have placed
>   One of the five-cent vases I bought in Greece.

(*He stands up suddenly*)

>   Ah! I bumped the desk—
>   The vase fell off. It's fallen down to the courtyard below!

(*A full or half-size* ARTEMIS STATUE *falls & crashes center-stage. As it crumbles, it speaks.*)

252

ARTEMIS STATUE:

    I am Artemis, goddess of birth, death, virginity, hunting and the moon!

EDWARD:

    You look beautiful in that pink dress.

CHRISTINE:

    Thank you! You gave it to me.

EDWARD:

    Oh? When?

CHRISTINE:

    I think in 1952.

EDWARD:

    I should buy you a new one. I will! Ough! pain!

(*He clutches his side.*)

CHRISTINE:

    Are you all right? What was it
    That fell?

EDWARD:

    The little vase.

CHRISTINE:

    Oh go and get it.
    I can probably fix it.
    Listen. I have something to tell you. I'm going to have a baby. Are you
        glad? We can afford it, yes?

SIRACUSA

EDWARD (*he sits on a stone*):

    My mother's favorite, aged eighteen, I while away my time
    Beside Arethusa's lovely fountain. She went underground for miles
    To escape her unwanted lover, or *he* went underground for miles to get
        close to her—
    As water, for miles and miles—

I forget which the story was, but I, in any case, now I am going
To visit my poor cousin Lucia, Lucia Caranotti.
She is confined to a balcony that is like a cage, it has wires all around it.
    This is to keep her safe.
She has a mental disease for which it is said there is no cure.

LUCIA:

    Ay! ay! ay! ay! ay!

EDWARD:

    At least, here in Siracusa it is believed that there is no cure.

PADUA

CHRISTINE:

    My voice, my talent for opera don't keep me from being lonely.
    Always surrounded by people, and by people singing, and to feel so
        alone—

EDWARD:

    This polenta is wonderful!

OTHER YOUNG MAN:

    Yes, it's best eaten with rich meats, such as game—boar, pheasant—in
        cold weather, in winter, in Italy.

EDWARD:

    You who seem, somewhat less than I am, giddily optimistic,
    You who are careful and superbly informed, do you see that woman,
    That young woman with her face full of glory over there?
    Do you see her, or am I really having an illusion? I could fall in love with
        her!

OTHER YOUNG MAN:

    I think you're going to see her tonight at the opera.
    She's Lucia Banvelli, a new star.

EDWARD:

    If only I could speak to her!
    But I am stuck to this table—here!

CHRISTINE (*sings a few long lovely notes*):
> Sono sola! sola! sola!

VENICE

EDWARD *as* TOLAVON:
> I'm black. I have a violent temper.
> I am, I hope, a great painter.
> I am Tolavon. They call me "The Moor of Venice."

ISABELLA:
> I am Isabella, the Venetian woman he loves. And who loves him. God
> help us!

(*She sits down to pose for* TOLAVON. *As he paints her portrait, he talks about his life.*)

DUCA DI DURO (*entering*):
> I'll buy it. Here are seventy million lire this deal is finished.
> I'll hang my daughter's portrait in my palace, on the side the sun shines
> on.

TOLAVON (*later*):
> I'll go see Isabella—and my painting!

(*Palazza Duro.* TOLAVON *goes in the Palace and comes out with his painting, which he angrily slashes to pieces with his knife.*)

TOLAVON:
> I found her with another man!
> Revenge! Vendetta! I should have killed them!

(*Pause*)

TOLAVON (*sitting in a caffè*):
> Isabelle found me and explained. The man was her brother. She hadn't
> seen him for years. I'm a fool to have such a short temper! But, well, I've
> made it up to her I think. And I've painted a new portrait of her, better than
> the first one—in some ways—although in other ways probably not.

ISABELLA:

Othello! My husband and my lord!

TOLAVON:

Keep up your bright swords, for the dew will rust them!
There would have been a time for such a word!
Put out the light and then put out the light.

ISABELLA:

Othello, walk with me.

TOLAVON:

Wait, Isabella! Stand there,
Just there. With that dewy
Palladio behind you, you look
Wonderful! I'm going to
Paint you there!

ISABELLA:

Ah, benedetto moro! Have your way!

BEIJING

EDWARD:

I'm going, with my wife, tonight, to the Tango Palace!
There is very little to do in this city
At night. Even holding hands in the street is forbidden.

(*He takes* CHRISTINE*'s hand and an* OFFICIAL *intervenes*)

OFFICIAL:

As you have just said. It is forbidden.
But you may hold one another in an accepted way at the Tango Palace.

EDWARD *and* CHRISTINE:

That's where we are going.

OFFICIAL:

It would be reasonable to find some practical use for the enormous network
of air-raid shelters built underneath the city's streets to protect the
populace from nuclear explosions.

256

(OFFICIAL *walks to another side of the stage and becomes a* SECOND OFFICIAL)

SECOND OFFICIAL:

Other possibilities having been found for one reason or another unacceptable, the state has decided to accept and to act upon Proposal 115-A, namely that the bomb-shelter network be slightly revamped to serve as tango palaces, five in all, places for the people to dance.

EDWARD:

Aside from our plain existence and our traditions we have little to entertain us.

CHRISTINE:

Dancing will be fun!

EDWARD:

At least we'll try.

(*He and* CHRISTINE *dance. Then they are chased away by the* OFFICIAL.)

OFFICIAL:

The tango palaces did not last long. There was a seepage of gas which made occupation of the shelters dangerous.

EDWARD:

The state could fix it, but there are other priorities.

OFFICIAL:

Here is one of them: elimination of dogs.
Get rid of your dogs. Kill them.
There is not enough food in Beijing to waste any of it on useless animals.
Therefore get rid of them. This order is absolute and absolutely final.
Disobedience will result in imprisonment.

CHRISTINE:

This would be a good time to revive the Tango Palaces—
To provide Beijing's people some pleasant distraction when there is
sorrow in many houses—

OFFICIAL:

Neither policy will be changed.

CHRISTINE:
How did you suddenly get so friendly with the manager of the hotel?

EDWARD (*secretly a little pleased*):
What do you mean?

CHRISTINE:
I mean I was upstairs for five minutes and I came down and you two were talking together as if you had been sharing each other's feelings and ideas for years.

EDWARD:
Oh I don't know. He started talking about his daughter who lives in the U.S.

CHRISTINE:
I see.

EDWARD:
Am I being criticized?

CHRISTINE:
A little bit. I suppose so. Yes.

BLOIS

EDWARD:
This is where Ronsard met Cassandre Salviati.
He wrote a thousand sonnets about his love for her.

CHRISTINE *as* CASSANDRE:
I am Cassandre.

EDWARD *as* RONSARD:
Would you like to dance?

CASSANDRE:
Volontieri. Gladly. I'd like to dance.

258

RONSARD:

> Do you know how many poems I will write to you?
> Do you know how many times I will see you?

CASSANDRE:

> No, I don't. Tell me the answer to each one.

RONSARD:

> I don't know either, but I know I will write
> A great many. And as for how often I will see you,
> That is up to you. I'd like to see you an infinite number of times.
> How old are you?

CASSANDRE:

> I'm fourteen.

RONSARD:

> Oh. That gives us a great number of times!

(*pause*)

> Yet now, after only a few months,
> I hear that Cassandre has married!
> Oh, love! Heavy is my heart!
> I'll write her, though, great poems—a thousand of them.

CASSANDRE (*thirty years later*):

> I wonder if he thinks of me now,
> All the same . . .

BEIJING

EDWARD *as* OFFICIAL:

> Please. Drive me to my office.

CHRISTINE *as* CHAUFFEUR:

> Yes, I will.

(*to herself*) Look how many thousands of people are in the streets,

> Even hundreds of thousands, even maybe already millions
> In the early morning streets. It is barely five o'clock.
> Millions! I am one of them, chauffering this car!

OFFICIAL:

Can't you make any better time?

CHAUFFEUR:

Time is against us because the people are for us.
Notice how they swarm around the car.

OFFICIAL:

Drive straight through them.
I don't mean that you should harm anyone by running over him
But do try to make way. Tomorrow we must start earlier.

(*In the street as they pass walks an agèd retired* UNIVERSITY PROFESSOR. *While the car is stalled by bicyclists, the* PROFESSOR *speaks, though the* OFFICIAL *does not hear him*)

PROFESSOR:

I am en route to the Pharmacy to buy powdered rhinoceros horn, a sovereign remedy, supposedly, for preserving potency into the furthest old age. I, however, don't use it for this—O burst of bright sun!

(*The sun breaks through the morning mist. A* DOG, *or an image of a dog appears stage left*)

I give it to my illicit and beloved dog, my chihuahua Wo Keechung, to keep him alive. Fourteen months ago all dogs were banned. But I have kept him, in spite of the edict. For this, my loved one, I'd gladly risk my life.

(*The* DOG *disappears. The* PROFESSOR *goes into the Pharmacy. The car starts moving again.*)

OFFICIAL:

I have good news to give to the Magician. We are going to renew his contract after all. He doesn't have to wait until September. I will give him his new contract now!

MAGICIAN:

I wonder if he will ever come? My contract will run out!

OFFICIAL:

Bo Hung! We have finally arrived! Traffic was a disgrace. There must be

fifty million people on the streets. But I have good news for you. I have
Good news for you. I really do!

MAGICIAN (CHRISTINE):
And what is the news?

OFFICIAL (EDWARD):
Your contract has been approved—for another year.
We have to find every Antonello da Messina in Sicily.

CHRISTINE:
Melissa will come, too. And your parents?

(*both leave*)

NEWARK

(EDWARD *as* IVAN, *a 56-year-old Russian man, enters agitatedly.*)

IVAN:
I want to hold on to Ekaterina, my wife! I met Ekaterina in Germany. She
and I were both prisoners of war. She had been captured, as a civilian, from
her native city of Leningrad, and brought to Germany to work in a factory.
They needed workers. So many Germans being killed. Work people must
be brought in from abroad. I was a colonel, in the Russian Army. I was not
captured. I surrendered. I was given an order to move my regiment
forward to a place where I knew, and the Commandant knew, that they
would all be killed. I was unable to carry out this order. I could not kill all
my men. They trusted me. I surrendered to the Germans. Then I also am
working in the same factory. Where I met Ekaterina. She is twenty-five
years younger than I. The Germans permit us to marry. When the war is
ended, we come to the United States. Here, too, I am working in a factory.
My English isn't good enough for a different kind of job. Ekaterina speaks
English perfectly. We have a son, five years old. Now she wants to leave me.

EKATERINA:
If he treated me differently I would not want to leave him. Do you know
that I have never been to a restaurant? I have never been to a movie. He is
too jealous to take me out. He thinks someone will see me, fall in love with
me, and take me away. Or that I will fall in love with someone else.

CHRISTINE (*as* HATHOR):
>Osiris, I'm concerned about the boat.

OSIRIS:
>I'm coming. What a job it is
>Each time we welcome a new person to the Land of the Dead!

TET:
>It's amazing that there is still room for them!

HATHOR:
>Finish the rigging. We haven't much time.

OSIRIS:
>You're tough. Hathor, beautiful and tough. But very beautiful with your
>>cow's head all the time.
>By the way, I haven't had time to think to find out,
>Who is it we are welcoming today?

HATHOR:
>Today we welcome
>Someone who stumbled on a step that was hidden in the sand
>At the Temple of Osiris-Pik.

OSIRIS:
>Oh, one of my temples!

HATHOR:
>Exactly, Osiris! And as he stumbled, a scorpion bit him,
>A deadly scorpion. That is why he is coming to us now.

EDWARD:
>I dream I am walking along a dusty white road with a bird-headed
>>individual.

(BIRD-HEADED BEING *comes out and walks with him*)
>I am ferried across a river on a boat lying flat on my back, wrapped in cloth.

(*He is wrapped up and laid down on the flat wooden bottom of a boat; then he gets up.*)

I am welcomed by animal-headed people, and handed an ivory staff.

HATHOR (*gorgeously dressed in blue silks*):
   We welcome you!

EDWARD:
   Why, you are Christine! the young woman on the boat!

TET:
   Welcome, to the Land of the Dead!

EDWARD:
   And you—you are the pilot!

OSIRIS:
   We are honored to welcome you here!

EDWARD:
   You—the man who takes tickets on the boat!

(*The real* TICKET TAKER *appears and hands* EDWARD *a* STAFF, *with which he immediately strikes and knocks down* OSIRIS *and* TET. *He takes* HATHOR *by the arm.*)

EDWARD:
   I want to stay with you.

HATHOR:
   Yes, I'd like that, too. What else do you want?

END

A NOTE ABOUT THE AUTHOR

Kenneth Koch lives in New York City and teaches at Columbia University. His books of poetry include *One Train, On the Edge, Seasons on Earth, Days and Nights, The Burning Mystery of Anna in 1951, The Art of Love, The Pleasures of Peace, When the Sun Tries to Go On,* and *Thank You.* His short plays, many of them produced off- and off-off-Broadway, are collected in *A Change of Hearts* and *One Thousand Avant-Garde Plays.* He has also published fiction—*The Red Robins* (a novel) and *Hotel Lambosa* (short stories)—and several books on teaching children to write poetry—*Wishes, Lies and Dreams* and *Rose, Where Did You Get That Red?*

He received the Bollingen Prize in Poetry for *One Train* and *On the Great Atlantic Rainway: Selected Poems 1950–1988,* both published in 1994.

A NOTE ON THE TYPE

The text of this book is set in a film version of *Ehrhardt*, a type face deriving its name from the Ehrhardt type foundry in Frankfurt (Germany). The original design of the face was the work of Nicholas Kis, a Hungarian punch cutter known to have worked in Amsterdam from 1680 to 1689. The modern version of Ehrhardt was cut by The Monotype Corporation of London in 1937.

Composed by Graphic Composition, Inc., Athens, Georgia
Printed and bound by Quebecor Printing, Fairfield, Pennsylvania
Designed by Harry Ford